Lucy English was born in Sri Lanka and grew up in London. She is a novelist and performance poet, first winning the Bristol Poetry Slam in 1996. She has performed world wide including The Edinburgh Fringe, Austin International Poetry Festival, Wordfest in Calgary, The Cuirt Literary Festival in Galway and has toured South East Asia for the British Council. She was a finalist in the first BBC radio 4 Poetry Slam. She was one of five poets chosen for the UK wide *Temptation* tour in 2005 and was artistic director for the *Exposed* tour in 2006. She co-wrote and performed the acclaimed multi-media spoken word shows, *Flash* (2010-11) and *Count Me In* (2013-14) with The South West Collective. Lucy is a Reader in Creative Writing at Bath Spa University where she teaches performance poetry. She is currently researching for a PhD in Digital Writing. She lives in Bristol.

with love

Lucy English

I would like to thank all the audience members who have laughed, cried or talked to each other during my performances. I would also like to thank my family and friends. It is not easy knowing a poet.

Prayer to Imperfection
Poems 1996-2014

Lucy English

Burning Eye

This edition published by Burning Eye Books 2014

www.burningeye.co.uk

@burningeye

Burning Eye Books
15 West Hill, Portishead, BS20 6LG

ISBN 978 1 90913 627 4

Cover Painting *Totterdown in Technicolour*
by Emily Ketteringham
Copyright © Emily Ketteringham
www.em-k.com

CONTENTS

THIS IS A PERFORMANCE POEM

This is a performance poem
and it starts with a statement,
sometimes political but usually factual,
such as, "Today my cat died,"
and it is followed by another, qualitative statement
implying my stance on the matter.
Which could be comical, cynical –
"Today my cat died and I didn't give a toss."
Or showing my caring nature, "Today my cat died. I cried."
Or even absurd, "Today my cat died. I am a fish."

I will then continue
and give you carefully crafted vignettes,
little scenes from everyday life, cunningly wrought
and presented in such a way
that you, the audience, will develop a strong identification
with me, the poet
and the subsequent bond will be a shared experience,
where I, the poet, will give you words and images to digest
and you, the audience, will feed off my energy.
This will of course vary,
(depending on my voice intonation and body language),
which will influence your interpretation.
My poem will have several layers of meaning,
but you will feel satisfied,
(depending on your intelligence),
even if you only get the saucy joke in stanza two.

I will then draw you in, astounding you
with complex language patterns,
intricate narrative structures,
definite rhythms which will become more pronounced,
and throbbing,
like a reggae beat,
using the voice
as the chief
instrument

in the language of struggle.
And more throbbing and pulsating!
Leading you gradually, but surely,
to the final climax
of tightly clenched words moist with meaning!
(I will use plenty of sexual metaphors.)
And even moister, positively dripping
I will hold you on that high plateau of verbal ecstasy
nudging out the last drops of your concentration.

Then, as you and me are overwhelmed with experience,
my voice will become slower and deeper
each word soaked in profundity, spoken slower and quieter.
I will sometimes use repetition.
I will sometimes use repetition,
and then you will know
and then you will know.

That the poem has finished.

TAKE ME TO THE CITY

Ah, ah, ah, ah.
Take me to the city.
Because the city is dying
like an old man alone on the sixth floor.
I can hear him next door, breathing,
or is that the balloons going over?
I can hear him coughing, or is that a car starting up?
I used to see him in the cafe opposite the tower blocks.
He never spoke.
He poured whiskey in his tea staring at his bacon sandwich.
His face was grey but he looked up and leered, brown teeth.
I wore a black plastic jumpsuit. I unzipped it.
But I was too expensive.

I walked to Tescos where the motorway meets the river.
Above my head, one stream flowing on concrete pillars.
The other, beneath my feet,
black and weed logged under like a sewer.
At least the brambles were still growing.
I wore nothing, but my fear of forgotten places.
Where buddleia grows on walls
and willow herb grows rank beside the rubbish bags.
The smell of water and one shoe.
Why always one shoe?
I do not know the stories of these places.
Houses with steel curtains and bricked up doors.
Sparrows in the roof fly through missing tiles.
So many empty buildings.

Ah, ah, ah, ah.
Take me to the city.
Because the city is heaving like lovers on a hot night.
Stuck with sweat and other bodily secretions.
And I shall be touched by a lover's hands.
Because my hair is Leigh Woods,
and my face is the downs with bumps and pits,
and my neck is the football pitch.

My breasts are the trendy drinking dens
down Whiteladies road,
and my belly is Broadmead,
unstructured and in need of a re-fit.
Here is Bedminster where the slippery river runs
and fig trees grow by the sides.
And my knees must be Totterdown raised up high,
and I suppose my toes are Whitchurch.

Ah, ah, ah, ah.
Take me to the city, because the city is ready to give birth.
Stretched open now and panting, ho, ho, ho, ho,
We are waiting. Push, push, push,
and it's coming! Yes! A new one! Push!
In a most unlikely place,
A little city with perfect tiny shops and people.
It's just like its mother,
and it's here to amuse us.

Ah..
Cute baby cities, there's a new one every day pushed out.
Here's one up my street with a car park.
Here's one in my garden looks like "The Galleries".
Here's one in my matchbox so small you can't see it.
Cellular cities,
each one bustling with impulses.
Dying, splitting, dividing, growing, giving birth to
another one.
So many rows of babies, with white faces.
With screwed up eyes and red open mouths wailing.
And each one waiting to be fed.

THE COMPANY OF POETS

Stuff the job!
I don't want to be discussing funding proposals
and where to put the coffee machine.
I want to be in the company of poets,
because poets only work when they want to
and they never work when they're tired,
and they never work when they're hungry.
And they forget to eat when they're working.
They say, "Pour me a whiskey, I'm depressed!"
They say, "Pour me a Tequila, I'm happy!"
When they run out of paper they write on bus tickets
or on the backs of envelopes which you throw away,
and they scream, "How could you! How could you!"
But they always remember it again and better.

Stuff the shopping!
I don't want to stare at cheap half cucumbers
and twenty three sorts of cheeses.
Darlings your Mummy's gone AWOL,
because she want to be in the company of poets.
Because poets dance on their beds when they're happy
and they shout at cats when they're depressed.
And they're upset because they want babies,
when they haven't got boyfriends.
And they're upset because their girlfriends
are having babies and they don't want them.
And they're upset because they've got babies,
sweet cuddly babies
and they want to write about them all the time,
but they know that is boring.
They're upset because they are babies
and who's going to look after them?

So they will turn to the company of poets,
because poets say,
at four in the morning, "Life's a banana!"
and you know what they mean.

19

Because poets say, "I had this weird dream I was a cactus!"
and you had it too.

Because poets wear clothes that don't fit them.
Because poets wear shoes that are scuffed down
but they look like a million dollars
and spend £60 on a tee-shirt.

Because poets spoil themselves rotten.
And they can't sing, but they try to,
and they can't play the guitar but they always do,
and they can't paint but they'll give you their paintings
and they can't cook, but you'd better eat it.
Because poets contradict themselves frequently,
because life, friends, is contradictory
and confusing, don't we know all know it.
And what's love got to do with it,
it's just an emotion said the joker to the queen.
All along the watch-tower.
I'm a sex machine. Get down and do it, you know,
doing it like a sex machine.
Yeah, baby, yeah, after all, you're my wonderwall, all, all.
When two becomes one.
Rose thou art sick and the invisible worm
that flies through the night has found out thy bed
of crimson joy and his dark secret
sandwich does thy life destroy.
Where Alph the sacred river ran
in caverns measureless to man
down to a sunless seaside holiday.
With the ape man, the walrus, bo, go, da, go,
helter skelter, bus shelter.
It's a far, far better life I go to than I have ever known.
It's a far, far better poem I have written
than any other poet has ever done!
And I shall stay in the company of poets,
because poets are never original.

They know everything's been said before
but they're going to say it again.
In case you didn't hear it the first time.

LIAR

I'm a liar. I'm a fake.
My hair's dyed. It's a wig.
I'm 62 years old.
I'm made of silicone.

This leg is rubber, you'd never guess.
I'm bionic. I'll live to be 200
but my brain is as sharp as steel.
I take smart drugs every ten minutes.
I can do the Independent crossword.
I can translate ancient Greek to Egyptian
and back again.
I can speak Croatian.

I'm a liar. I'm a phoney.
I'm not trendy. I'm tricking you.
I don't wear these clothes at home.
I wear fluffy pink slippers and a blue nylon housecoat
and curlers in the bath.
I have gold taps and deep pile shag maroon carpets.

I like Sky TV. I like Oasis.
I like Val Doonican and James Last
and military bands and highland pipers.
I wear a kilt. I'm really Scottish, och aye.
I'm really Irish. I'm really Belgian.
I'm really Japanese. I'm really a Christian.
I'm really the virgin Mary.
I'm really a virgin.
I hate sex. It's messy and sticky. I hate men.

No I don't.
I am a man and I'm British and I love my country.
I raise the flag on Sundays. I like shooting pheasants.
I don't believe in poverty.
I was in the army. I was in the S.A.S.
I was in the Falklands.
I was in the Gulf war. (Both of them.)
I was in the Gurkhas.
The regiment. The Queen. God bless her.

I am The Queen.
I'm The Queen's twin sister surgically altered
and hidden away for years with a peasant family
in a bungalow in Woking
And I have now come to claim my title and start a war.

No I haven't. I'm a liar.
I'm an alien and I have come from another galaxy
and a loop in the time-space continuum.
Because we are the guardians of the universe
and we have been watching you for centuries,
and you have disappointed us.
No you haven't.
I love you. I love you all. I love all of you.
We are full of love.
Feel the love. Can't you feel it,
flowing like a river between us.

I'm a liar. I don't love you.
It wasn't an orgasm.
I was looking at the ceiling and I saw a spider
and I shouted out, "It's huge!"
I don't love you.
I love my window cleaner.
I love that man over there
and I want his babies and I want to get married
and live in a truck
and be happy and free and uncomplicated.

And his dick is bigger than yours.
Let's be friends. You will always be my friend.

I'm a liar. I didn't write this.
Ted Hughes wrote this. He did. He did.
The last poem before he died.
I'm a liar. I didn't write this.
My eight year son wrote this
because he's a genius and I keep him locked in his bedroom
and I make masses of money out of his poems.
Masses and masses of money.

No I don't.
I'm a liar.
I wrote this. This is the truth.
I wrote this and I will get paid bloody nothing for it.

GREEN

This is my shirt catching the light.
A princess dress, a silky cloak
of the queen of the river.
Wind across long grass crushed velvet.
Summer rain on the plane trees.
Still water in the canal.
Bright pondweed. A frog on a stone.
Emerald cat's eyes. Go... go... go...
go walking through the woods in the early evening.
Nettlebed near the riverbank. Deep water,
swimming under. A sea mist.
Shadows as speckled as fish.
My shirt catching the light
in a storm sky of lime juice.
Vine leaves on the balcony.
A salad bowl of August.

DO NOT GET TO KNOW ME TOO WELL

Do not get to know me too well
because I want there to be some kind of mystery.
I travel alone and do you remember
corridor trains with compartments like a sitting room?
Tartan seats of uncut moquette.
A net rack to put your suitcase in.
Black and white photographs of Paignton sea-front,
Salisbury cathedral behind glass.
When you open the door I shall look at you,
frostily, if I want you to go away,
or with a smile, not too eager,
and you, shall sit opposite me.
We shall share this journey, not talking much.
Smiling, meeting eyes,
looking at the countryside flashing past the window.
"Do not lean out of the window," it says.

I travel alone but we can share this journey
although you do not know where I'm going,
and I won't tell you.
I want there to be some sort of mystery,
because I think you'd get tired
of my archaic memories.
My stories of aunties and cream teas.
A dream I had about a rainbow.
A lavender party dress I used to wear.
When you see me looking dreamy.
You might think I'm being creative,
having magical thoughts,
working out some kind of mystic puzzle.
But I'm not.
I'm just sitting there,
watching the countryside,
flashing past the window of an old fashioned train.

ONCE WERE LOVERS

Once were lovers
but now I'm not sure what we are
when talking stops
and the space between us waits
like breath on a cold day.
What I used to do was hold out my hand
because talking was difficult for you
and feeling seemed to jam it up.
But I don't touch you now, and the white space hangs
until we find another sentence
or look at a newspaper, anything, that fills in time.

And we were lovers who touched,
a hand on a knee,
a finger in a finger.
This I remember, not sexy, but a contact.
There you are.

There you are, now, creased,
If I squeeze your arm or kiss you goodbye.
I see it on your face, embarrassment at remembering,
once were lovers.
Do you remember when I came round,
I just got in through the door,
and you pushed me up against the wall,
you couldn't wait?

I have this fear
I will not feel again so strong,
look in your eyes and know exactly what you felt.
We used to lie there and be that gone.
So blissed out.

I've sat through your girlfriends
and seen you treat them
with tolerance, acceptance, and yes, tenderness.
I have to admit that,
but not passion, like we felt.

Once were passionate lovers.
You tease me. You say, "He fancies you,"
and I say, "I know, I shagged him all last week."
What can I say? He doesn't feel like you.

I'm not talking reconciliation here,
but I feel such strange things.
I want to stand in front of you
and say, "Let no one hurt this man,"
because you're vulnerable and also daft
getting in such scrapes.

Once were lovers.
I wanted you to feel good about yourself
and proud.
you never did.

You don't feel good about yourself
and I know this.
You don't say it and it stays
in the frosty space of unsaid things
I wish would melt away.
I wish would be a sea
where thoughts could swim
and you could catch my thoughts
and say, "Hold me," and mean it.
Then nothing would stop me.

LOVE AND SEX

This one's about love and sex.
And you know all about sex.
Oh you, can twiddle and tweak.
And fuck the girlies until they squeak.
And fuck them to the back end of next week.

But let me tell you about love.
For you, an Oh! I feel so hot sort of thing.
Heart skipping, sliding down your thighs
Tingling candy floss drug to fluff up your brain.

It could be.
But I feel something else.
Let me tell you about my long ago tiny child.
A drop of milk on his cheek.
A pearl tear dropped from me.
Untasted in his full up sleep.
I have been kissed right through
but I'm still not empty.

Let me tell you about your father.
Who used to chuck you up so high
you were flying.
And carried you around the garden
pretending tigers and elephants in the roses,
is now asleep.
The crossword on his lap.
His glasses coming slowly down his nose.
Your mother brings the tea, forgets the sugar.
You don't want them to get any older.

You're with your friends.
And the talking stopped with the last can of Guinness.
But nobody says it's bedtime.
The room is warm and smoky.
You live even in the corners
and with the dust under the sofa.
But nobody says it's bedtime.

I want to tell you about quiet love.
You don't recognise expecting noisy stuff.
You are bare and awkward.
You, who have shagged on beaches and in cars
and round the back of some seedy pub, you told me once,
by the dustbins.

You come back for this.
Silent pushing.
I'm in your eyes. Makes you uncomfortable.
You hold my hand. Are you lost?
You could be.

And we are plunging.
I'm thinking of the mud at low tide.
Sliced with river channels.
The water lapping the sides.
And all of it smooth rounded gleaming in the sun
and humped like a whale's back.

And we are smooth mud water
salty tasting in my mouth.
Filling though to me, through to me
The deepest river bed of us.
My dear.
I want to tell you about love and sex.
When you lie with your head on my neck
and I hold you inside.
It feels like you belong there.

DRIFT (With J. Words and Ethos Sphere)

I have ten fingers to play this game.
I have nine lives, but I've only got eight left.
I have seven mysteries
and seven brothers who are wild swans,
but you can't see them.
I have six, six, six, tattooed on my forehead,
but only when I'm angry.
I have five alive senses and I hope I'll never lose them.
There are four horses at my apocalypse,
greed, power, lust and pride.
I have three blind mice, and three wise men
in my holy Trinity.
There's two, you and me babe,
on different sides of the battle field.
I have one. One heart. One love. Do you want to share it?

What are we afraid of? Let's drift...

...into all our different selves,
not just drift but push into the corners
and go beyond.
And where shall we go? Where can we go
that hasn't been visited already?
Tell me what it's like.

...cocooned chrysalis visions when the last snow melted,
quilted, guilt laden, coupled up cuffuffel,
falafel soaked truffle, ruffled revel, swivel,
swirly souls, sorted, pensive,
present tense,
I can't sit on the fence,
when there is only grass...

Greener on the other side and all flesh is grass
cut down now to its roots.
Bare earth moment waiting for the touch,
of Spring, and we need growth,

from the soil, the earth our slave,
thank you for the love you gave,
like a full on rush at a rave – ah!
New waves we cannot sink under.
New fire cannot burn us now.
New wind cannot unwind us now.
Cannot slave the earth to us.
Unslave us ravers. Savers of bad behaviours.

...nature breed nurture, mother earth elemental rapture, animal
instinctive, chemical resistancy, tinsel town
come round for a cup of tea,
no... really...
drink this elixir of perception,
stands for environment creation,
eat this vital statistic enriched toastie,
tasty crisp and Crunchie-cookie monster,
magic moments in love with you...

Unaware what I'll do next. Conjuring pictures of pleasure,
this subtle treasure, a thought shared is an idea doubled.
Trouble unlimited.
What are we afraid of, what are we afraid of?
When the boundaries crumble,
tumble down around our ears
and leave us naked.

Drift...

Set your own limits,
because the bubble skin
is too fine.

Inside, looking through rainbows,
seems soft, protected.
But the flimsy wall will pop,
and there you are,

bare, where it pierces you,
and your eyes hurt from seeing
things sharp and harsh.

You need your own gauzy distance.
A clothing,
between your world and the mind.

Drift...

I feel I've been so many lives
there must be many more,
and though I'm tired and want to kiss the ground
like wet blossom on the pavement
melts away. I feel I have to find a new version
to open out my mind.

And I want to be perfect.
A white marble angel in a graveyard,
solemn and compassionate,
standing through the years.

And I want to be perfect.
A shot silk piece of sky
to catch the sun come up
and toss it into morning.
And I want to be perfect,
like the first star shining
before the lights come out
above my city.

SKETCHY

This one's sketchy, so I will draw the outline
and you can fill it in.
Five hot people on your doorstep and you don't know them.
They don't know you, they hardly know each other.
Different coloured snooker balls bumping,
falling down the pockets.
And what's in your pocket?
A telephone number, a piece of string,
a baby's sock. A wedding ring.
We're here to make connections.
Touched by your generosity. This is Brighton on a Saturday.
We want to give you what we do.
We want you to understand and be part of the picture.

This one's sketchy, so you can join the dots
and what shape is emerging?
A cafe, sea blue walls and moo cow chairs.
A piece of colour in a street of colourful people.
This is where it happens, the place where we speak.
Are you listening? Did you think poetry could do this?
When we laugh and cheer and even cry.
Did you think words could do this?
We've gone beyond politeness now,
hear the feelings, hear the emotions,
hear the meaning.
Meaning, when you think, "Oh yes, I felt that!"
It's worked.
It's worked. We weren't sure it would
and now we can celebrate.
Open out our tightness because we have touched you.
This is Brighton on a Saturday night. This is what we do.

This one's sketchy, but you can choose the colours
and paint them in.
Here's a moon toking on the clouds.
Here's a shingle beach
as loud as the splashed up party gang.

And where is the party?
Waiting for something to happen.
Waiting for something to happen....

And here it is.
Rolling down the beach,
a luminous plastic wave,
an enormous roll of bubble wrap.
With a line of dancing girls.
Let the mad romp begin.
After creamy hot chocolate of course and now who's tired?
He is.
And who wants to jump on bubble wrap all night? They do.
Different colours down different pockets
and mine's a sea blue duvet, thank you.

Your front room's a soft mattress to mattress
sleeping place
and we are the grown ups waiting for the children,
smoothing out their comfy beds. Let's be grown ups.
Let's talk into the night about grown up things,
like how tired we are.

But the morning tide washes in the flotsam
and here they come, the pop, pop, pop, party gang,
plastic seaweed, bladerwrack, bubble wrap crew.
You won't believe it!
And they did this...
A man tied to a lampost with a rubber sheep.
And they did that... lost the credit cards.
And they went there... all over Brighton
and drove over a rabbit.

This one's sketchy but let's stretch the paper
over the frame of words and make a kite.
Who's got the worst hangover? They have.
So let's take your baby to the beach

and make little houses out of stones.
Let's talk about the things
we haven't done yet in our lives
and how complicated it all is with partners,
children and no money.
Let's make big mad plans
because this is Brighton on a Sunday
and the sun has got his hat on
and is strolling up the beach.
Let's all play.
Let's put our worries on the kites.
Sketchy people, beached up
and the bubble wrap has all been cleared away.

This one's sketchy, a scribble
so let's put in the ands and buts and make a sentence
and say, "Thank you."
We know each other a few days better
and I will come back because I like you.

Driving home a different way.
Sketchy people in a car, getting more sketchy by the hour
and what's in my pocket?
Hot chocolate cream, the seventh wave,
a bubble street, and a dead rabbit.
We shall take back fragments,
fill in the colours, join the dots,
stretch the paper and write it down
so you can be part of the picture.

Which is always changing.

STILL LIFE

This is still life.
Early morning, white sheets and a white wall.
Curtains flapping at the window
in the attic of my grandparents' house.
You are sleeping next to me.
And you are my brother, eight years old.
When you wake up I will tell you my dream.
I will tell you about thunder crashing and high mountains
and a palace with four hundred steps.
And you will say, "Dreams aren't like that.
They're about missing trains, lost rabbits and latin prep,"
and I'm on your side of the bed.
But now you are sleeping
in the early morning, white sheets and a white wall.
Curtains flapping.
This is still life. Shh, don't move. Shh, don't move.

Sun on my face
on a Sunday morning
in a college room smelling of cigarettes.
And you are sleeping next to me.
And you are my first lover
the wrong man, my boyfriend's brother
and I've got a hangover.
When you wake there'll be recriminations
and whose fault was it anyway?
But now you are sleeping
in the early morning, white sheets and a white wall.
Curtains flapping.
This is still life. Shh, don't move. Shh, don't move.

The sun on a pot of geraniums.
The smell of a slept in bed
and a black bird singing in a bush outside.
A cottage.
And you are sleeping next to me.
And you are my baby's father

and the baby is asleep at last.
My breasts are tender and heavy.
My body feels floppy and loose.
A milk sow with eighteen piglets.
Lover, baby, lover, baby, lover, baby, piglet.

But you are both sleeping
in the early morning, white sheets and a white wall.
Curtains flapping.
This is still life. Shh, don't move. Shh don't move.

A hand on my back and a foot against mine.
A breath on my cheek.
A breath in my ear. Wheezy breathing
and you are sleeping next to me.
You are my six year old son with asthma
sleeping the fitful sleep of a sick child
hot and sour smelling.
Outside a bird's singing.
On a Sunday morning. White sheets and a white wall.
Curtains flapping.
This is still life. Shh, don't move. Shh, don't move.

A hand on my back and a foot against mine.
A breath on my cheek.
I'm stretching, turning towards you.
And you are
You. It's you.
I was dreaming about thunderclaps.
A bird's singing outside.
There's a pot of geraniums.
My body feels soft.
Your hand's on your cheek.
The city is waking.
Your shoulder is warm.
Our toes are touching.
My breasts feel tight.

And you are sleeping
On a Sunday morning.
White sheets and a white wall.
Curtains flapping.
This is still life.
Shh, don't move.

POETRY IS THE NEW DISCO

Come on down it's a Tuesday night,
go to a slam feels alright.
Claire's a babe, Glenn's so cool.
They know the score, they know the rules.
Some poets fade and some survive.
Some will ride and some will slide.
Boy meets girl. Girl meets boy.
They'll find themselves a piece of joy.
You know how it's going to go,
because poetry is the new disco.

P. O. E. T. R. Y.

P – it's popular
O – it's awesome
E – it's excellent
T – it's totally excellent
R – it's really sexy
and Y – it's for YOU!

P. O. E. T. R. Y

P – it's pretentious
O – it's opaque
E – it's existential
T – it's tangible
R – it's a religion

Come on down it's a Sunday night.
Go to the Coffee Company feels alright
Drink your Kenya, drink your wine
chat to Polly, she's so fine.
When those Next Up poets do their thing
it makes my bell ring.
Boy meets girl. Girl meets boy.
They'll find themselves a piece of joy.
New York, London, Brighton, Bristol.
The whole world knows poetry is the new disco!

P. O. E. T. R. Y

P – it's pullable.
O – it's over the topable.
E – it's excitable.
T – it's totally incredible.
R – it's really unbelievable
and Y – it's for YOU

P. O. E. T. R. Y

P – it's passionate
O – it's orgasmic
E – it's extra orgasmic
T – it's tantric
R – it's rude-tasmic
and Y – it's for YOU!

OLD

You're 40, I thought you were 28 or something. I mean you're not covered in wrinkles and you're not fat and baggy. You've got three kids that's amazing and the oldest's 16, I mean my baby sister's 16. Wild! I was saying to my mate Justin, I call him Jus, he's the one over there with the glasses, I was saying that Claire Williamson looks pretty horny I wouldn't mind a go on her but she looks hard to get and he said, "what about that other blonde one, she's not that old."

But 40, I mean that's pretty good really that you still get up and do all that sex poem stuff. I think it's really cool that in Bristol older people go out and enjoy themselves, where I come from, Basingstoke, when you go out I mean you never see anybody over 26 except sad slappers and all the others stay at home with their kids. But 40, that's amazing! I mean Bristol's like that isn't it? I mean I went down the Fiddler's the other night with Jus to see a Cuban band. Wild! And there was this woman dancing and all that and I mean she was about 60, and hey! What if somebody got a bit drunk and chatted her up and copped off then they woke up the next day and they were in bed with somebody as old as their granny. Nightmare!

But 40's not that old I mean that Glenn he's over 40 and he's a mean cool dude, I bet he cops off with that Claire, he's old enough to be her dad. Crazy! But perhaps she likes older men, perhaps she likes something a bit more mature, well, I don't stand a chance do I?

Hey, I was thinking, what if you hadn't told me, I mean I was going to invite you back for a smoke, you know a 'smoke', and to listen to some stuff by that DJ at the Lakota, but you're probably too old to be into all that and hey... what if we had got really stoned and Jus would have crashed out, he always does, and what if we had got a bit horny on the sofa and then I'd said, "let's try the bed," my rooms a bit of a tip and all that and the light doesn't work so I wouldn't have been able to see you properly, and what if we had done it all night, and in the morning I'd said, "I never thought I'd get off with a 28 year old," and you'd said, "but I'm not 28 I'm 40!" Nightmare!

I mean you're old enough to be my mum. Wild! I mean, fancy my mum getting up and doing poems. Unbelievable!

LONDON

London. London.
Maybe it's because I'm a Londoner I still get sentimental
about red buses, Big Ben
shopping in Oxford Street and
they're changing guards at Buckingham Palace.
I love London. There's so much to do.
There's so much to do you don't know what to do.

Well, you could go
to a little chrome and wood coffee bar in Soho,
where the music's so loud you can't think
and for £19.50 you can have a light lunch
the size of a small biscuit.
Where all the women are trendy and beautiful and a size four
and if you manage to speak to them
and ask them what they do they go all languid
and say, "I'm in films,"
but if you press them further you find out
what they actually do is work
in a dingy office in Shepherds Bush
for a company that makes corporate videos
entitled "The Future of Springe Throckets"
and the men in the coffee bar are all drop dead gorgeous
with identical twatty haircuts
but don't even bother talking to them,
they're gay.

London. London. What to do in London?

Well, you could go to a museum.
The Science Museum is full of science,
the Natural History Museum is full of people.
You could go to the V&A which is pretty empty,
especially on the sixth floor
in the middle of Chinese porcelain
and you're only up there
because you got lost going to the loo

and there's one other person,
an ecstatic old codger who's saying,
"Gosh, it's Gung ho Pung dynasty!"
So you ask a fossilised attendant who directs you through
mediaeval woodwork,
nineteenth century lace
and Samoan religious artifacts,
then you're lost again and you're in the plaster gallery
and just before you wet yourself
you're trying to answer those two great unanswered questions:
How on earth did they make a plaster cast of Trajan's Column
and why is Michelangelo's David's dick so small?

London. London. There's so much to do in London.
Especially at night when everybody else is doing it as well.
You could go to Covent Garden and see the latest lavish production
of 'La Traviata'
cunningly set in twenties gangster Chicago.
For a hundred and fifty pounds.

Or you could go to a film. But the two films
you want to go and see are booked out until next April
so in the end you make do with American Wank part 7
full of exploding everythings and blood everywhere
which makes you feel sick
nothing to do with the bucket of popcorn
and the bucket of Coca-cola you've just consumed.
You stagger out into the foyer
which is full of Japanese tourists
taking pictures of each other
and into the street that is so packed you can hardly move
and somehow you get talking to a drunk Glaswegian
who asks you for 50p so he can get a train back to see his blind,
dying, one-legged
mother in Kirdkudbright.
A train to Scotland for 50p? He is ill.

London. London.
Why is it that when you live in London you live in Watford
and all your friends live in Walthamstow
so when you go and see them
all you can think about is getting the last train home,
and you nearly miss it,
because all of a sudden
the Bakerloo line has been shut down,
and at Baker street you leap into a carriage, the doors close
and there you are
with six masturbating weirdos and a man who keeps saying
Have you discovered Jesus?
Have you discovered Jesus?
Have you discovered Jesus?

London.
Maybe it's because I'm a Londoner I still get sentimental about
urban poverty
slap bang next to high security luxury flats in Docklands.
Beggars under Hungerford bridge.
Nose to tail traffic on the North Circular.
The wrong sort of leaves, or is it snow
that closes down the whole underground network
and everywhere you go chaps with woolly hats on
trying to sell you copies of the bleeding Big Issue.
Maybe it's because I'm a Londoner
that some chirpy cockney chappie says to me,
"If you park your bloody car there once bloody more
I'm going to bloody smash
your bloody face in."

Maybe it's because I'm a Londoner
I don't live there anymore.

A TO Z OF BRISTOL

A is for Avon which doesn't exist.
B is for Smiles Beer which gets us all pissed.
C is a council without any dosh.
D is for the docks which makes Bristol look posh.
E is for East Street where everything's cheap.
F is for festivals, there's one every week.
G is for the Great Western Railway of Brunel's engineering.
H is for Horfield, a riotous prison,
and I is an inmate on the roof jeering.
J is for juggling. Bristol has balls.
We also like K, kite flying and climbing church walls.
L is for London where we used to play in the grime and the dirt
'til we moved away
to M, mingle with mountain bikers at the Mud Dock cafe.
M is also for Montpelier, dodgy after dark.
N, nice people live in Clifton, Westbury and Snyed Park.
O, 'orrible people live in tower blocks up Barton Hill,
in Hartcliffe, Lawrence Weston, Knowle West and Pill.
P is for pubs, and they're everywhere.
    There's the Star and Garter, give it a cheer.
    The Brew House, The Cadbury House, The Flyer's got poets,
    The Shakespeare in Totterdown, does anyone know it?
    The Fini's for phonies, the Shed is for poseurs,
    The Nova Scotia's for gaffers with sun burnt noses.
Q is Queen square, Georgian and pretty.
R are the roads which mess up this city.
S is the Suspension Bridge and the Second Severn Crossing
wonderful sites completely free.
The rest you have to pay for
when we have "The Festival of the Sea"
T is a tramp, he sits up Park street.
He has a small puppy, isn't it sweet?
U is the University, which one, we've got two.
I love students. Why? Don't you?
V are the visitors who pour in each year,
we're a cultural capital isn't it clear?
They hang round the docks then they go to view,

the W, Wallabies, the nyraXs, the Yaks,
which you can see too
all properly looked after in Z Bristol Zoo.

REALLY BORING

I want to be really boring.
I want to spend the whole night snoring.
No more soft drugs.
I want to drink hot chocolate in Care Bear mugs.
No more toy boys, no more love toys.
I threw them all away, they didn't work anyway.
I don't want a sex life. I want to be a housewife.
I want a nice little hubby,
with a beard and he's rather chubby.
I want to live in Swindon.
At least I'd get my shopping done.
I want to be really boring.
I want to clean the bathroom every morning.
I don't want to go to Goa and get a sun tan all over.
I want to stay in bed and watch the telly
and do the garden in my wellies.
I want to be uninspired.
I want to be retired.
I want to be brain dead. I want to listen to Simply Red.

I want to be really boring and wake up every morning
and know that I'm not cool and I haven't got a swimming pool
and a private gym to keep me fit and trim.
I want a big fat wobbly tummy
and stop pretending I'm not a mummy.
I won't shop in Red or Dead
I'll buy my clothes at Littlewoods instead.
I want a patio. I want a video.
I want a mobile phone. I want a Wimpey home.

I want to be really boring,
and go to car boot sales on Sunday morning.
I don't want to have to think.
I want ruched curtains in pastel pink.
I want to be anaesthetised.
I'll get my children baptised.
I want to believe in God, he sounds like a happy sod.
So you can all go to Hell,
to some Cheltenham Literary Festival.
And I shall go to Heaven.
I'll go bird watching in Devon.

EXCUSE ME

Excuse me I'm not a man.
But I'll do the best I can.
I shave my head and wear big boots.
I won't giggle, I won't wiggle and I won't look cute.
I won't chatter and I won't yap.
Excuse me. I can rap.

Rap, rap, cat flap, read a map, take a nap.
Here we go...
Rap rapping, hand clapping, back slapping,
foot stamping, wheel clamping.
No more cake baking. I'm making lots of noise.
Because I'm up here with the biggest of the big boys.
Raunchy, paunchy, punchy, out to lunchy.
Thank God it's Friday I want my Crunchie.
I like football. I like cricket. I like rugby
and I can understand it.
I play badminton. I play squash.
I play tennis. God, I'm posh.
Like a Tory MP.
I say, I'm in the minority.
Arrogant. Intelligent. Belligerent. Ignorant.
Like a man.
Beery. Leery. Lairy. Underarm hairy. Fall down the stairy.
Like a man.
In a nightie. Great big fairy drag queen.
Like a man.
Mean machine. Post teen. Know what I mean.
I've got a Motorguzzie and it's red.
I've got a pit bull and it's dead.
I play snooker. I play pool. I wear black leather
and I'm so fucking ice cool.
Like a man.

Look at me. Yes I can. I can be like a man.
I can shout. I can yell. I can sweat. I can smell.
I'm becoming like a man. Mind numbing like a man.

Bongo drumming. Bare bumming. Bare chesting.
Green investing. Caring sharing poncho wearing.
Health shops. Flip flops. New agey goatee beard.
Mars in Pisces. Mega Weird.
Like a man.

Train spotting. Fly swotting. Wife swapping.
Stamp collecting. Metal detecting.
Bridge erecting. Drain inspecting. Rat dissecting.
Self correcting. Self protecting.
Like a man.

Hang gliding. Tank driving. Granny knifing.
Planet polluting. Infant school shooting.
Like a man.

But, excuse me, I'm not a man.
Excuse me.
I'm a Woman.

WHAT'S THE STORY MORNING BOLLOCKS?

I'm the excellent fuck.
And you're in luck,
because you're getting on well with the excellent fuck.
I'm squeezy. It's easy to please me.
I will act out all your fantasies.
But just before you push up my knees.
Could you please ask me,
those questions I want you to ask me?
Let's forget about bodies. Could you ask me where God is?
And do I believe he's a she,
an earth mother to nurture us all with the spirit of love
on this tiny planet?
And do I like carrots
served with chemicals that kill us slowly?
And do I care about dying
when there's lives not lived properly?
Can you please ask me those questions I want you to ask me?
Like, is Tuesday nearer to Monday or is it a Sunday
that's nearer to Monday?
And what colour is Sunday?
Is it gold or blue or apricot pinky salmony red,
and when I'm in bed
What do I think about before I start dreaming?
And how do I know when I'm dreaming?
And can two people dream the same dream at the same time
and if they did what would it mean?
And do I like double chocolate, chip chocolate ice cream?
And how could I describe that taste so accurately
you would know exactly
what I was talking about?
Your mouth would go wet
with the thought of the thought I was thinking.

Could you please ask me
what it feels like when I come?
Do I feel filled with exquisite waves of delicious emotion?
Or do I just feel numb and slightly damp

and my leg's got cramp.
And how do I feel about you when you hump me
all bumpy bumpy.
I'm squeezy. It's easy to please me.
I will act out your weirdest goat rubber fantasies.
But could you please ask me
what do I see when I sneeze,
and have I ever been to a cheese factory?
And why do I collect shells and never throw them away?
And what did I see when I first saw the sea
and ran straight into it
not knowing it could be dangerous?
Then screamed and screamed because it was terrifying.
And what's the first thing I remember?
And if I can remember that
why can't I remember the minute before?
Can I remember learning to walk?
Can I remember learning to talk?
Can you think without words? Describe with your fingers?
Gasp with your eyes?
Shout with your prick, make a story with bodies that has hundreds
of endings
and all of them happy?
And can caterpillars be happy?
And if they were how would you know?
And if they were sad how would you know?
Can you please ask me those questions I want you to ask me?
Like, is bread raw toast?
And what's the most amount of chocolate
I've eaten in one day?
And when did I last eat snow?
And if I was happy how would you know?
Can I do cartwheels? Can I stand on my head?
Can I do back flips? Do I wear socks in bed?
Do I like raw fish?
If I had three wishes what would they be?
Have I ever been caving? Have I ever been raving

stark staring mad?
And if I still was how would you know?
Can I describe the difference in taste
between roast goose and roast duck?
Do I believe in destiny or is it just luck?
Can you please ask me
before you tell me
I'm an excellent fuck.

MAKE ME A MODERN CHRISTIAN SONG

Make me a modern Christian song,
and one that you can sing along to
with a tune that isn't too complicated
and words that hardly ever rhyme.

And fill it full of pleasant cliches
like "God is love" and "Heaven is above",
and, believe it or not, Earth is below,
and we will
all let love work.

And don't mention anything like sin
or have words like death and destruction creeping in.
Do not discuss spirituality
or good and evil and their duality,
because these days we are all too ignorant
to have a sensible debate about religion
but say words like humble and downtrodden,
because after all this hymn is modern.

Make me a modern Christian song
and one that you can strum along to
on your guitar or bang your bongo drum
because it looks good on Songs of Praise,
and in the middle put in plenty of surprises
just in case we are all falling asleep.

Make me a modern Christian song
and one that is twelve minutes long
so if you forget the words then you can hum,
dum di dum, God is our chum
and that is why we have come to church.

MY WORST THINGS

Girls in white dresses with black lacy panties.
Unexpected visits from uncles and aunties.
Silver toe-nails. Paul McCartney and Wings.
These are a few of my very worst things.

Over large families with overlarge arses.
Yes, I'll admit it, I hate the working classes.
Pig ignorant, ugly, bigoted and mean.
These are a few of my very worst things.

Just to be fair I also hate yuppies
with ghastly dinner parties in designer conservatories.
Schnitzel with celeriac, darlings, nouvelle cuisine.
these are a few of my very worst things.

On rainy Sundays listening to the Happy Mondays.
In Post Office queues.
I simply remember my very worst things
and then I know I'll pull through.

Rottweilers, dobermans, chihuahuas and spaniels.
I hate dogs. I also hate Paul Daniels.
Trendy vicars, I want to shoot them.
Aerobics instructors, I want to nuke them.
Car ads, food fads.
Anything with the Spice Girls.
The Royal Family and Candle in the Wind. Shut up!
The Last of the Summer Wine. I bloody hope so.
All that pseudo cutesy Scottish Irish rot.

Riverdance. Why?
Wonderbras. GWR.
Celebrity babies
and I don't care if everyone gets rabies
when I'm in the bath and the telephone rings.

Oh, my god, I hate everything.

THE RELATIONSHIP SELF ASSESSMENT FORM

Now our relationship is over
And you have gone away.
I'm sending you this relationship self-assessment form
So you can have your say.
Please fill it in and send it back as quickly as you can
For it will come in handy
When I find another man.

(Please circle one of the following.)
1. Was I psychic? Compassionate? Indifferent? Or a bitch?
2. Did I make you happy? Drive you nuts? Or satisfy an itch?
3. Was I too short? Too tall? Too fat? Too thin? Too wide? Too small?
Too big?
4. Were my manners, exquisite? charming ? adequate ?or resembling
a pig's?

Did my body a) look like venus b) or some potatoes in a sack?
Are you a) desperate for my company b) or do you never want me
back?

1. a) Do you cry into your pillow? b)Do you wank yourself to sleep?
2. a)Did I remind you of your sister? b)Or would you prefer a sheep?
3. a)When we made love did you see stars? b)Or did you just see
Betty Blue?
Please tell me darling. How was the relationship for you?

What shared activities did you prefer. a) A country walk.
b) A cup of tea. c) All night drug crazed clubbing,
d) or a game of Monopoly?

1. a) When I met your mother was I respectful and polite?
b) Or did I declare her décor tasteless and told her how to put it
right?
2. a)Did your brother like me? b)Or did he classify me insane?
3. a)Did you father say I was gorgeous? b)Did he say I had no brain?
4. a)Did I admire your Auntie's knitting? b)Did I stamp on it and
scream?

5. a)Did I park your car in a ditch? b)Or did I park it like a dream?

Did I A) adore you? B) Boss you? C) Nag you? D) Bore you?
E) Enthrall you? F) Thrill you? G) Spill you? H) Chill you?

Was I an angel dropped from heaven?
Or a bug to make you sick?
Was it too short or far too long?
And I'm not talking about your dick.
Do you miss me? Do you still love me?
Or do you want to move to Honolulu?
Please tell me darling. How was the relationship for you?

ANOTHER WALES

Communication crosses all bridges.
Thoughts like cars streaming into another Wales.
Your territory different from mine.
We don't speak the same language.
And you are mountains, valleys, rows of stone walls
and I am suburban hinterland of a spreading city.
Such nicely trimmed gardens my dear.
Such beds of roses.
Two car families.
Crossing bridges with communication.
Not spoken. A hand moving. A look in an eye.
Are words necessary when underneath us
boils the river meeting the sea tide,
washing in a brown flood across the mud flats?
Where long legged sea birds
call out to nobody.

LATER

Later than this time I will sleep at last and dream I hope
because dreaming is my only last
creative act which still surprises me.
I don't have to worry out words or plot
or character development, structure, sequence.
Dreams have none of these.
Changing. Even the characters change.
Faces, locations, but the feelings are real.
I can wake up exhilarated,
despondent or unnerved by something
on reflection seems so harmless.
A door opening onto a corridor with bare walls.
Why does that fill me with sadness?

Later I can leave this rational frame
and empty myself into the shifting world
where the surface of a table has such shining intensity
and clouds blow into solid shapes
and a thousand steps lead to a palace on a mountain
and stars move across a sky of rainbows
and a white horse stands and listens to me.
A door opens onto a corridor with bare floors.
One naked light bulb,
brown walls and silence.

MORNING, MORNING

Morning, morning.
Silver blue fish hardly ever disappear into sleeping
but greeny turtles rapidly become
something retarded on a plate.

Never wipe your armpits with a fish paste sandwich,
don't cross the road without leaving your handbag at home.
Darkly letting nothing a bit like sunshine.
This is what my hair should look like
when I'm shagging enough.

Morning, morning.
Run a bath deep into tomorrow's dream time.
Stick your nose into this it smells like pleasure,
and raise the water table please because
blankets are mostly for falling backwards.
Pink is a concept for excellence,
folding over a sticky flap envelope I never posted
to my grandmother who didn't live in Wales.
Did I ever tell you about her?
Sketching: orange on black a swirly question
different from a broken green outline of a
fat shape looks like a heart with trailers
a burning kite on a black sky of paper.

I don't care who you are or where you're from
as long as it is now. Sunday morning 5th October.

LANGUAGE

You say vegetal red globule. And I say tomato.
You say Earth's gonad. And I say potato.
You say translucence veil and I say cling film.
You say a night at the opera and I say I'm done in.
Globule, tomato, gonad, potato.
Let's call the whole thing off.

I say Massive and you say Debussy.
I say sorted and you say excuse me?
I say chill out and you say relaxation.
I'm a human and you're an alien.
Let's call the whole thing off.

You say Swinburne and I say Cooper Clarke.
You say devoid of daylight and I say dark.
You say in the arms of Orpheus and I say crash.
You say nature's harvest and I say stash.
Lets call the whole thing off.

I say they're my friends and you say delinquents.
I say manic and you say omnipotent.
I say freedom and you say post-modern.
I say dripping and you say sodden.
Let's call the whole thing off.

You say Aphrodite's bower and I say cunt.
You say manna of the gods and I say spunk.
You say if mucus be the food of love, and I say boring.
You say once more into the breech dear friend
and I say I'm done in.
Bower, cunt, manna, spunk.
Let's call the whole thing off.

WISHING FISH

Wishing fish clock turn the time.
Blow your bubbles for the children to catch and wish,
spinning in time.
I wish. I wish. I wish I could have new ideas
every hour, every half hour
as fast as you.
A new thought every minute,
spinning the yellow balls down the tube
and a mouse pops out of its box
and the fish blows a bubble.
Another word out of my mouth.
I wish. I wish. I wish I could always remember
I walked through the park in the Autumn
where the wet leaves stuck to my shoe
and the trees were planted for dead people.

The blackbirds on the grass like the lives of my children,
ready for flying.
And the apples on the trees like the dreams of my friends,
ready for picking.
And the stream round the wall, flowing into the weir
a true place for a wishing fish to blow bubbles.
I wish. I wish. I wish
I could always remember when I walked through the graveyard
where the new trees split the tombs in half
bursting from the hearts of the buried.
When I walked through the yellow, red, yellow, gold, brown
orange, berry red blood Autumn
and I wasn't sad.

WINTER POEM

I wrote this one in the Winter
when the sky was as grey as concrete
and there was no sunlight for three weeks.
It wouldn't rain and it wouldn't snow
and we lived all day in a blanket.
And the evening started at four
and we never opened the curtains.
So here's to the Prince of Darkness
who comes to me in the night
in a suit of blackest velvet.
I never see his face but his nails are carefully manicured.
So here's to the Prince of Darkness
because I won't listen to his lies
when he tells me I'm worthless and I won't make it.
When he whispers to me in the cold
that I'd rather be dying than living.
And this is a new year, and this is a new year.

And I wrote this one in the Winter
when the sky was a lavender pillow case,
a pillow case made out of silk,
and the streets were as white as a duvet,
and the air was as sharp as lace.
We watched the sun rising on three hundred bedroom windows.
So here's to the Angel of Light
who holds my hand in the morning
and stays with me without talking.
And this is a new year, and this is a new year.

And I wrote this one in the Winter
when the sky was as black as slate
and the word written on it was thunder.
It was a strange weekend.
The wind was tearing off branches.
We ran through the streets between hailstorms
and knocked on friends' doors, "Let us in! let us in!"

A red sofa and a gas fire.
Be quiet, the baby's sleeping
in the stillness of a back room.
In the stillness of a Sunday.
Outside the wind pelted the windows
and the thunder shook the chimney.
So here's to the Mother of the Earth
who can still scare me with a fierce storm.
I hid all night in my bed
as she shrieked up and down my street.
So here's to the Mother of the Earth
who poured rain for three days on my garden.
Who tugged up the green tips of crocuses.
Who pulled out buds on the maple.
And this is a new year, and this is a new year.

I said, forgive me my arrogance,
because I've discovered I'm good at something.
When I stroll down the street in a long coat
I'm pretending I know who I am.
And I said, forgive me my sadness.
It's an old scar but it can still hurt me.
And I said, forgive me my impatience.
I want to run, I've had enough sleeping.
And I said, forgive me my hesitance.
I going to jump in the water.
And I said, forgive me my clumsiness.
When I trod on your foot at the party
Who said emotions were tidy?
When I stroll down the street in a long coat
I'm pretending I know who I am.

And this is a new year.
And this is a new year.

THE BIG CRACK

There's a bruise on my leg.
You didn't hit me.
But your hipbone pounded against my thigh.
So much energy in a small space.
What were we trying to prove?
That we still cared about each other?
That we still wanted each other?
Or did you just like the feel of the wet crack?

The crack.
For the fun of it, the laugh of it, the joy of it.
The big crack.
So sweet and compulsive you can't resist another shot.
Another crack, another scramble up the rock,
to reach the top, the spin, the buzz, the high.
Clinging on with your hands in case you drop.
The crack in the pavement I mustn't step on
or I'll get bad luck.
The cracked mirror, the seven-year curse,
unless I wash the pieces in a natural spring,
bursting its way from out of the earth.
Oozing mud, through a cleft in the rock,
the split, the rent.
Something I saw through the flap of a tent.

The crack of the whip.
A sudden slash across my face.
A streak of hurt, a blow, a snap.

The crack in the ice.
I've fallen through to dark water
so cold I've frozen.
And I was on the hillside watching the sunset
dancing with the drummers, swaying to the beat,
the thrusting beat at the base of the spine.

My bruise,
Yellow and purple.

There's a sunset on my leg
And I'm waiting for it to fade.
To the pink smooth skin of my own new dawn.
My smooth skin.
My sustenance.
My innocence.

SEND ME A MAN

Send me a man who can love me for who I am.
Send me a man who can hold me in his pocket like an egg
and I know I won't break.
Send me a man who can climb me like I'm a mountain.
Send me a man who can love me for who I am.
Send me a man who knows about empty deserts,
moated castles and bus stations.
Send me a man who wears stars on his shoulders.
Send me a man who carries air in his hands.
Send me a man who can put up shelves.
Send me a man who can love me for who I am.
Send me a man who wants to play
with my train set on a wet Sunday.
Send me a man who knows sex can be playful.
Send me a man who has planted a garden.
Send me a man who has jumped over a wall into a garden.
Send me a man who can swim underwater with his eyes open.
Send me a man who knows sex can be devastating.
Send me a man who can love me for who I am.
Send me a man who knows money doesn't grow on trees.
Send me a man who finds a ten pound note in the park.
Send me a man who knows the value of the one eyed jack.
Send me a man who gives me his best friend
to be my best friend.
Send me a man who loves his father.

Send me a man who can love me for who I am.
Send me a man who says, "Are you ready?"
Send me a man who has read *Swallows and Amazons*.
Send me a man who went looking for the goddess.
Send me a man who found his children.
Send me a man who can love me for who I am.
Send me a man who loves roses, chocolates and cathedrals almost as much as I do.
Send me a man who knows about things I know nothing about.
Send me a man who knows nine months isn't a long time.
Send me a man who knows nine years isn't a long time.
Send me a man who knows death isn't final.
Send me a man who can love me for who I am.

PLAYING CHOPIN

Every good boy deserves fun.
And every good girl learns to play Chopin.
Three ferns on a table by a window.
A blue room and a black piano.
Convent girl with plaits. Red ribbons.
Her feet touching the pedals.
White socks. Brown shoes
and sister Lelia taps with her stick.
She's eighty two. Her face is a wrinkled rose petal.
The rest of her a black habit of diligence.
One, two, three. One, two, three.
This is the sad one in A flat opus 69 no. 1.
Good boys deserve fine apples.
But the convent girl cannot make it sing like it should.
A sad lonely lilt, she's struggling lento.
She tries again, con anima
and runs up the scales like a navvy in workboots.

All cows eat grass.
The black and white defeats her.
There are too many.
She's trying to catch them and make them notice
But they move away.

One, two, three. One, two, three.
Convent girl wants to do it dolce.
And here comes the song again
she wants to sing.
Battle ends and down goes child's father.

She's waltzing round the ballroom
in Vienna.
Swirling dresses flash in the candelabra.
Bare arms, bare chests and tiaras.
Two hundred hot perfumes dance to the sad growing tune.
She sees him as she turns.
Her head on the handsome Prussian.

The pale young man at the piano,
his eyes closed as he plays.
Playing this waltz for her.
He told her in a letter and he will die soon.
He is like a white lily,
waxy, repulsively perfect,
but she wants put her cheek against his
not the whiskers of the handsome Prussian.
Her cheeks are pink now.
She turns and turns again, she is flying.
One, two, three. One, two, three.
Poco a poco crescendo.
Father's child goes down and ends battle.
He opens his eyes and sees her.
He has brown eyes the colour of the mud
he will soon be under.

Convent girl in white socks plays the final glissando.
All three octaves.
She has never played it so well.
"Very good", says sister Lelia.
"Now let's try *Fur Elise.*"
And she does without a falter
because she is a few minutes older
walking across an empty ball room.

HOLY ISLAND

The clouds stretch far along the hills.
Grey shreds remaining of the damage.
Along the causeway seaweed's thrown
and on the island branches and broken tiles.
Last night this place was cut off by the storm.

We walk towards the castle and there's that feeling
of aftermath.
The red-blood sun of a winter's afternoon.
The sheep graze on unperturbed.
The sea birds cry unnoticed.
A thousand years of history undisturbed.

A monk tracing beauty on a parchment.
A feudal lord cold on his castle rock.
Ten black sailed ships on the horizon.
This island waiting for another shock.

You say, "I love this place."
And one hand touches the furthest shore.
The other skims the hill tops and the causeway.
This wild and grainy beauty in your arms.

You will always be for me this holy island.
Your head the castle looking out to sea
at the lonely Farnes.
Your eyes as brown as seaweed.
Your back the curved and pebbled beach.
Your chest the ruined abbey.
Holding the light of learning. The hope of love.

And I shall be the sea.
My eyes as grey as low tide puddles.
My hair as yellow as the sand.
And I shall be the sea
rolling in across the mudflats
to flood your causeway.

Cut off from the mainland you float on me.
Twice a day we shall be forever.
One place.

SLOW

This one's slow.
A drink in the garden on an August Saturday.
A bee kissing each open flower.
A cat's tail flicking in a puddle of sunlight.
A shadow moving down the wall.
A spider's thread floating,
timeless, pointless, random.
Thistledown caught by the rosebush.

This one's slow.
A steam train down a wooded valley in the rain.
A cream tea in Watchet.
a lacy doily on a patterned plate.
The scent of roses.

Slow:
An empty church on a summer evening.
Flowers by the altar shed petals on the floor.
Tombs worn smooth by centuries.
Silent as angels.
Slow:
A painted clock at the end of the corridor.
A Persian carpet in the back room.
Velvet chair by the window.
A child playing in the garden.
Slow:
A black and white film on Sunday.
A requiem for a lost day.
A long bath in the candlelight.
Slow:
Cloud busting in the stone circle.
The sheep are grazing quietly.
Slow:
A station waiting room in the suburbs.
The last train of the evening.

The last exam in a heatwave.
The last bus to Jaipur.
The last dance at the wedding.
The last night together.

A tap dripping in the kitchen.
A shadow moving down the wall.
A spider's web floating.
Timeless, pointless, random.
Thistledown caught by the rosebush.

AUTUMN POEM

This is the autumn of my life
and I shall walk through an autumn wood
and talk about quiet things
and feel completely understood.

This isn't a love poem.
It's a celebration of those moments, unexpected.
When I turn my head and something I didn't know was there
makes me stop and hold my breath with reverence.
A rainbow resting its soft foot
on your side of town, arching its back
across a tumble of storm clouds.
I look again. A shining with a mirror twin.
Two rainbows.

A magpie's back. Purple blue black strutting bird
in the sunlight of a city morning's waste ground.
Back luck. I turn my head and there's another.
Two magpies. Two for joy.

This isn't a love poem.
It's a celebration of stillness.
A single leaf turns spirals as it falls.
I'm dancing with the soft tug it took
to rest my eyes on apples melting in the grass.
Opening their hearts. Becoming softer, becoming sweeter.

I used to want a flash of silver and a bolt of turquoise
but now I know there are two hundred shades of grey.
And grey becomes brown like a moorland rock
speckled with the orange and green of lichen.
And the rain's a grey curtain drawn across the sea.

This isn't a love poem. But I will tell you

that desire   is the rain swept in from the sea
to soak you through completely.
      Wet.

And desire   is the body shape left in the grass.
You've gone but it's remaining.
Pressed.

And desire   is the breeze so soft you can barely feel it
but all the crimson trees
Let down their leaves.
      Shaken.

SHOP

I am a shop.
Because people walk in and say
Have you got any
lunch mum?
Clean socks?
Food. Always food.

I am a very small shop.
I am running out of stock.
I am up the highest shelves
and at the back of drawers.
Have you got any
patience, understanding?
Sandwiches, roast potatoes?
Cure for nightmares? Warm jumpers?

I am a disorganised shop.
I am often closed.
Especially on Sundays.
In the mornings I am full of sun
but by the afternoon
dark and gloomy.
People walk past and bang on my door.

Have you got any love?
Go away. I'm shut.

CITY EDGE

My house went walking in my sleep
and when I woke

I wasn't on the city edge.

The town below,
grey layers against the grey.
Green snake river to the station
and crouching trains.
Their hum rises
to cars and lorries.

I sometimes go down.
Watch sunsets on my street.
At night leave curtains
to see the lights.

The city,
fragile as it seems from here.
Never people filled.
Never concrete.

But today my house has slipped.
I've woken to a field.

Is so still.
Is so flat.

PAPER, SCISSORS, STONE

Smooth me out so plain and white
and write on me,
a poem, a shopping list.

Crease me, fold me, mould me.
Scribble on me, or paint.
Stick me on your wall.
Call me Art. Call me wallpaper.

Tear me up.
Discard me.
Burn me.

I'm sharper than you think
and jealous.
I'll snip off your hair.
Cut up your best shirt
and love letters.
Then I'll cut you.
I watch you bleeding.

I rise to mountains
and fall down oceans.
Fear me.

I'm under your fields and streets.
Make caves and houses.
Live in me.

I'm your temples.
Hold your religions.
I am the effigy.
Worship me.

GOOD FRIDAY IN IKEA

Jesus died for somebody's sins but not mine.

There was a four-mile tailback up the motorway.
Mothers, fathers, little children and grandparents.
They were all there.

Daughters of Jerusalem weep not for me
but for yourselves and for your children.
For behold the days are coming in which
they shall say blessed are the barren.

The Virgin Mary and the mother of James
liked the Ektorp sofa bed and the Bonde storage units.
But Joseph of Arimathea couldn't find the rattan chair called
Bomsund.

Under a hundred hot lamps the Magdalene
finally chose a low energy uplighter.
Peter and Beloved John bought plants, sheets, cutlery.

Five thousand trailed round the mock up kitchens,
pretend bedrooms and dining rooms
with Swedish books, fake fruit
and computers with no cables.
Your home could look like this.
A yellow sign said, Lack TV bench £49.
This is the king of the Jews.
There was a vat of cushions and another of dustbins.
Children cried. Parents fought.
There was a brief scuffle over a kelim.
Luke got lost among the flat packs.
The staff were over worked.
The restaurant ran out of meatballs.
And it was about the sixth hour
and there was a darkness over all the earth
until the ninth hour.
You find the best bargains just before closing.
Father into your hands I commend my spirit.

THE LAST CHANCE SALOON

This is the last chance saloon. Are you sitting comfortably?
It's the last chance saloon,
where you look in the mirror and there's another wrinkle
and your tits are heading towards your knees
and your bottom's already got there
and you've taken up Yoga classes.

It's the last chance saloon,
where you don't wear vest tops anymore
and you found something you really like in Littlewoods,
but you've just spent £38 on a fancy bra.

It's the last chance saloon,
where you don't go for promotion
because you want to spend more time on your garden
and you're seriously considering selling up
and moving to Yate.

It's the last chance saloon,
where you buy cookery books,
and gardening books,
and you fantasise about Monty Don,
fondling your primulas.

It's the last chance saloon,
where the high point of your week
is lunch at Poppy's tea rooms in Chipping Sodbury.
Tuna bake with extra salad,
followed by a cappuccino and a bakewell tart with no cream.
All in an atmosphere of stripped pine and fresh flowers
and a clientele whose average age is 74.

It's the last chance saloon,
where you stick photographs in an album
and write witty comments underneath.
"Me in a silly hat. Glastonbury 1999."
And the last time you had totally, glorious,
gorgeous abandoned sex,
was Glastonbury 1999.

It's the last chance saloon
where you watch with morbid fascination
old women hobbling up the street.
Where every twinge is cancer
and six people you know are dead already.
And you're not lonely,
you have heaps of friends,
but you have recently started talking
to your goldfish.

It's the last chance saloon,
where you know if you don't do it now
you know you never will.
'It' meaning scuba diving, rock climbing,
white water rafting, salsa dancing
and aromatherapy massage.
And a ticket to Bangkok costs £349
but you have just booked a mini break to Windermere.

It's the last chance saloon,
where you don't go to Ikea
because it's full of young families,
and you don't visit your sister
because her children are so beautiful it could make you cry.
And every month you want a baby.
But every month as you wash out the bloodstains
you know you're never going to have one
unless there really is such a thing
as the Immaculate Conception.

It's the last chance saloon,
where you don't mind
that he has buckteeth, and a beard, and a stamp collection,
and an unhealthy interest in rabbits,
and a mother who lives in Swansea.
You know
you could still fall in love with him.

THE WOMAN YOU KNOW

I'm fifth in line,
I'm cousin to The Queen.
I'm white sow mother.
I'm sweet sixteen.
I'm the pale virgin shrouded in snow.
I'm the ice cream girl, the woman you know.

I'm the battered wife with a bruised lip.
I'm the refugee, child on hip.
I'm the triple goddess by the standing stone.
I'm Greta Garbo and I vant to be alone.
I'm the skinny bitch who wants your job.
I'm the wealthy widow you want to rob.
I'm Miss Scarlet dressed to kill.
I'm the lap dancer. Your cheap thrill.
I'm your dancing partner, steady and slow.
I'm your best friend. I'm your best friend.
I'm your best friend.
I'm your best friend in line, the woman you know.

I'm the Next girl who lives next door.
I'm the Amazon warrior six foot four.
I'm the queen of swords slicing the air.
I'm Rapunzel and here's my hair.
I'm the traffic warden who's towed you away.
I'm the strict mistress you must obey.
I'm the housewife with a rubber glove.
I'm the child bride you always loved.
I'm the child in the street from long ago.
I'm your sister. I'm your sister. I'm your sister.
I'm your sister in crime, the woman you know.

I'm Delia Smith starting to cook.
I'm Virginia Woolf starting a book.
I'm Carol Vorderman doing her sums.
I'm Carol Nobody being a mum.
I'm the helpline worker. Can I help you?

I'm the black madonna dressed in blue.
I'm Kali Goddess who couldn't cry.
I'm the Chinese baby left to die.
I'm the dead princess in a pretty bow.
I'm your daughter. I'm your daughter. I'm your daughter.
I'm the daughter of Time. I'm the woman you know.

UNDER THE HEDGE

Where the sheep hide under the hedge.
The hedge a wide ditch and
the hazel trees creeping along the ridge.
Old men. Bent, covered in fur coats
Fern growing out of the pockets.

Fungi. Small saucers of gold.
Moon creatures in the dead bark.
Wet like a sponge.

Where the sheep hide.
Their wool rubbed along the bark
Leaving thin milk strands.
Spider's webs of fluff.
The dirt floor. It's all brown.
Leaf mould carpet moss on twigs.
And the rain. I can't ignore the rain
on my tent roof of trees. Tapping
on my paper. The writing smudges
into tears.
A robin sings and flies into the hedge
checking me out.
Singing little songs for me.
A wet sheep, curled in the dip
of a tree cave.
A tree tunnel.

THE LAST DAYS OF THE OLD YEAR

It's the last days of the old year.
I'm sitting here watching the rain fall
on the brown rooftops.
Looking towards the city
hiding in the mist like a future I can't quite see yet.

This time last year I had so much optimism
But all I feel now
is your absence. The child I never had and never will.
All gone, like the rain streaming down the garden
under the fence you painted.

You spent all day in the rain
laying the patio.
You put so much energy into this house.
Your home. Our home.

It's strange what I remember.
Hairs in the sink. I kept picking them out.
Your shoes as big as boats by the front door.
A green jacket in the hallway.
And the food you ate.
Organic rice with tofu.
Noodles and chinese fungus.
Miso. Seaweed. Peppermint tea. Soya milk.
It was healthy.
I grew plump on it.
Your plump bird in a velvet dress
folding up your boxers like a true gemütlich housewife.
I planted herbs and flowers.
Happy, plump and fertile.
So I thought.

It's strange what I remember.
Teas in Portishead. Country walks.
Did we spend all our weekends
walking through fields in the sunshine?

Cathedrals and castles. Lonely beaches in Northumberland.
It felt that when we were out walking
We were the king and queen of fairyland
and time slowed down to let us pass.
It felt what we had was a glimpse of perfection.
And it never rained.

It's raining now. Sheets of it.
The clouds are crying on this house. This garden.
You lying on the floor and crying.
I've never seen anybody cry so much as you.
Crying for the baby we never had
and the relationship draining around us.

It's the last days of the old year
I'm sitting here watching the rain fall
on the brown roof tops.
Looking towards the city hiding in the mist.
Looking towards a future I can't quite see yet
Like Orpheus walking out of the underworld
I mustn't turn back.
But I just have.

So now I am alone.
And I shall walk the streets at night alone.
And I shall brush my teeth at night alone.
And I shall sleep on my side of the bed alone.
Because inside I am alone.
And you, asleep,
up the other end of town.
Inside, I know, you are alone.

THE TELEPHONE BOX UP ASHLEY HILL

There's a telephone box up Ashley Hill
where I go and stand sometimes when I'm feeling down.
From up there I can see the allotments sloping
towards the terraced grid of houses in St. Werburghs
and the streets of Easton, Eastville and beyond,
the first fields just outside Bath. The ridge of hills

reminding me that the city isn't endless.
However stuck and messed up I feel,
when I stand there I know there are places
I haven't been to yet,
and people I don't know at all
are waiting for me as surely
as the clump of trees up Kelston Hill.

There's a telephone box up Ashley Hill
where I go and stand sometimes when I'm feeling down.
Because I've been in the rain up there.
When the rain dripped off my nose
and the hills disappeared in the clouds.
And I've been in the sun up there,
watching the heat rise off the dusty city.
and I've seen the view so winter white.
The curving hills like frosted crystal.

And I've been drunk up there.
Watching the stars slide across the sky.
And I've tripped up there.
Going to the moon with a ten pence piece.
And I've been up there with lovers
Kissing passionately banging against the phone box.
Or just held hands in silence
watching the sky grow red with sunsets.
And once and only once
I landed up in the nettles
in a dope fuelled tangle of lust.
Don't try it. I had a rash for days.

And a long time ago
I took a little boy up there
and we hung onto the railings
our coats flapping in the wind.
The spring wind pressing our eyeballs tight.
And I shouted, "Look, look at the view!"
And he looked, a solemn old man four year old
and said, "The sky is very big."

There's telephone box up Ashley Hill
where I go and stand sometimes when I'm feeling down.
To look at the view
and the big sky.

SWEET THING

She's a sweet thing and she goes all pink
when you whisper in her ear
that's she a tasty licky little snack.
And the way you squeeze her fingers and touch her hair
is so familiar.
Was it really only last week?
My bed still smells of you.
My sheets still have your stains.
When you last feasted on me.

And I am not a sweet thing I'm a hungry thing wanting more.
But I see there won't be any more.
Because she suits you.
Not wild and bold and unpredictable and mostly absent.
She's there.
Did you think I would flip my lid to see her?
So you could say, "Well it's all over, isn't it?"
But it's not over because we're starting out
on something you're not used to.
When we were, through the day,
Five or six times spunked. Tasting each other.
Coming electric.
You splice me.
Wrapped round each other talking nonsense.

And I'm a hungry thing. These are not my limits.
I'm a demanding thing. I wanted to feel you feel.

Look, she's laughing now. Was I so easily amused?
I'm an angry thing on an edge and I want to say to you
Jump. Jump. Jump away.
From trippies up the pubby. Cooky little din-dins.
Watchy little film-films.

She's looking baffled now. I'm not surprised
Because you have run away from me
and into this sweet pillow thing.

You're hugging her like a big boy hugs his mum.

Jump. Jump. Jump away and walk with me.
And we shall walk through the dark town.
The streetlights shining in the gold puddles.
We shall dance in the gold puddles.
Our boots making a whirlpool of noise.

We are children. We are beautiful.
We are meteorites kissing the moon.
Much more demented and sublime.
Than any sweet thing.

A DRY SUMMER

Summer is for nothingness.
The sky's a perfect blue.
The grass in the park has dried to mud.
This bus stop's a barbeque.

On Christchurch green
the bright young things are having picnics.
Girls in tight skirts sit down oh so carefully
trying not to show off their g-strings.
Tarquol and Damien are already drunk.
Hoorah for summer!

The woman with the moustache has a new boyfriend.
He squeezes her knee
in a tender gesture of possession.
They look so happy.
What's she got that I haven't got?
A moustache.
I'm not bitter, don't get me wrong
but if you poured me out
I'd burn a hole that was this deep.

I'm not bored, but if I slept anymore I'd be a silk worm.
I am bored.
I have spent the last ten minutes
watching a crisp packet blow up the street
whilst waiting for the bus to nowhere.

Things to do today:
Write a book.
Get a life.
Kill a bus driver.
Oh no, it's only two o'clock
and I have already done everything on my list.

I am bored. I am so bored I could eat my shoe.
I am so bored I could eat you.

What shall I do?
Shall I phone you up and ask you to come round
so you can shout at me?
What shall I do?
Shall I tell you exactly what I think about your search
for your perfect baby?
What shall I do?
Shall I talk to you in my spooky voice
so you will think I really am
the wicked witch of your imagination?

I'm not angry. Don't get me wrong
just don't stand too close in case I spontaneously combust.

What shall I do?
Shall I tell you a story
of when we walked along the cliff top
from Clevedon to Portishead
in the springtime when we still had hope.
I'm not unhappy, don't get me wrong
But if you put a tap in me and turned it on
the water wouldn't stop flowing.

But last night I was out.
In my lucky knickers and my push up bra
and my fuck me shoes.
I was down at the Prom Bar.
With everybody else.
And what were we looking for?

What am I looking for?
"What am I looking for?
Long given up on fame and fortune.
Who am I shouting at?
You'd rather watch TV."

(Not my lines but they were good ones.)

Summer is for nothingness.
A hot bus stop with no bus.
A city full of people not talking to each other.
A dry garden waiting for rain.

WASTING TIME (a poem for two voices)

Let's waste some time.
If you were a biscuit what sort of biscuit would you be?
Hob nobby chocolatey dip in my coffee, I think.
No, what are they? Crunchy, with those big bits of peanuts that stick in your teeth
and there's six in a packet?
I'm one of those. Definitely. Today.

Let's have a biscuit.
Let's eat all the biscuits.
Let's feed each other biscuits.

God, I'm covered in crumbs!

Let's not sweep up the crumbs.
Let's roll six joints and see who can smoke the most first.
Let's count the stains on the carpet.
That one looks like a rabbit.
No, a giraffe standing at a bus stop
and that one by the telly is an airforce blue bus
with only three wheels.

That's not a stain, that's my sock.
That's not a sock, that's my watch.
That's not your watch, that's where I spilled the coffee.

What is the time?
Time to clean up?

Let's not clean up.
Let's see how many different ways we can sit on this sofa.
Don't ceilings look funny when you're upside down?
Let's walk up the bookshelves and run round the lampshade
and open the curtains with our toes.
But I can't reach my tobacco.

Let's have another joint.
Let's have another another joint.
Let's have another, another, another joint.

Can you blow smoke rings?
Can you blow a smoke ring inside a smoke ring?
I like your mouth.
Let's snog.
Let's get our tongues all muddled up.
You taste of biscuits!

Let's get all sexy and chuck our clothes over the telly
and make mad stonking love on the sofa and on the floor
and all over the carpet.

Let's do it again but this time a bit more slowly.
Let's roll a joint.
Let's listen to something ambient for a very long time.
Let's not put our clothes back on.

Let's write down the names of everyone we've ever slept with and
count them!
Total combined score…72
That can't be right! You slag!
No, you're the slag. Six Traceys. Six!

Let's feel guilty.

Let's make some resolutions.
I will from now on respect all the women I sleep with.
I will get a job. I will do more exercise.
I will pay more attention to personal hygiene.
I will stop eating junk food.
I will read more. What's yours?

I will hoover the house twice a week.
I will recycle everything.
I will buy the *Big Issue*
I will from now on respect all the men
and the women I sleep with.

What?

Let's have an interesting discussion about sexuality.
Let's go upstairs. Let's do it.
Let's do it in a new and different way, and I saw a picture in a book
somewhere, now where is it?
God, this room's a mess!
Sod that, let's do it the same old way
but it still feels pretty good.

Let's roll a joint.
Let's stare at the ceiling.
Let's count the number of leaves on that plant.
Let's have a cup of tea.

I need to make a cup of tea
so I can remember I actually live here.
Let's have some more biscuits.
Let's drink up that whisky in the cupboard.
Let's listen to some dance techno fusion dub jungle music very loud
and dance.

Yeah, let's dance!

Let's try on all my clothes.
God, you look stupid in that dress.
Let's paint our toenails green.
And dance some more,
let's go in the garden and shock the neighbours.
Let's shout "We are the cosmic transvestites!"
Sod mediocrity! Sod tediocraty and aristocracy!
Astronomy! Astrology!
I'm an Aquarian with a Sagitarius moon-ocraty!
Please Translate?
No obligation for a translation station.
Translate?
Slate my thirst. Milk shake first.
The first to quake is out.
Translate?
Fellate?
Fuck! My head! I need my bed!

Oh god, no more sex!
Yes, now on the stairs. Mind the hairs.
No more sex. Oh alright.

I'm making mad stonking love
to a man with green toenails in a dress.
I love you! I love you! I love you!
Sorry.
I wasn't supposed to say that.

Let's get embarrassed.
Let's not talk.
Let's finish off the whiskey.
Let's fall asleep on different sides of the bed and wake up
dreary, smeary and bleary.
Ready to waste another day.

THE SEVENTIES WERE CRAP

The coolest decade with the coolest sounds?
What is this nostalgia for the era that taste forgot?
I shall debunk the myth.
I know, I lived through it.

The seventies were crap.

Cutting edge fashions? Not in my town.
I wore tank tops knitted by my gran.
In sensible maroon or donkey brown.
Black lace up shoes and navy slacks.
Crimplene shirts and pac-a-macs.
The seventies were crap.

Innovative décor? Not at Auntie Jean's.
Swirly brown carpets and a three-piece suite.
Six floral patterns in orange and lime green.
Nylon net curtains with a frilly trim.
A crocheted dolly to put the loo roll in.
The seventies were crap.

Groovy music? Yes, if I liked Sweet.
Heavy rock annoyed my mum.
She didn't like those progressive beats.
She listened to Cliff Richard all day long.
Or a nice catchy Val Doonican song.
The seventies were crap.

Opportunities for women? My teacher hadn't heard
that I could be anything other
than a nurse, or a teacher, or a dolly bird.
Or a nun. And if I got a job I'd give it up one day.
All women leave and have babies anyway.
The seventies were crap.

Fish fingers. Baked beans. Sandwich spread and Spam.
Margaret Thatcher milk snatcher.

Nixon. Watergate. The War in Vietnam.
Rail strikes. Power cuts. Close the coal mines down.
Jimmy Saville. Benny Hill and dirty northern towns.
The seventies were crap.

SHOPPING

You wouldn't think it was so difficult to find a pair of trousers.

I mean, all I wanted were some trousers for work.
Black, well fitting, reasonably stylish.
No frills, washable, the right length for ankle boots,
low cut,
flat front with a bit of stretch for those PMT days.
You know. Simple trousers.

So I went to TK Maxx. Great. Hundreds of black trousers.
And they were all a size eight.
Now, I'm not fat but I'm not a size eight.
I am normal. I have a bottom and a tummy. It wobbles.
I have children. I like cake.
So why aren't there any trousers that fit me ?

So I went to Marks and Spencers.
Great. Dozens of black trousers.
Now the problem is do I want kick flares, or low rise,
or comfort fit, or straight or baggy or suit cut?
How they hell do I know?
I just want a pair of black trousers!
So I go into the changing rooms with six pairs.
(I am only allowed six pairs)
of selected size fourteen trousers.
And guess what.
Two don't fit me and two are too big and two I don't like.
So, I go back and change the small ones for bigger ones
and the bigger ones for smaller ones
and the ones I don't like into ones I do.
Ten minutes later. Three don't fit me.
One is two big and three I don't like.
I never could do maths.
Twenty minutes later I have mistakenly put back the one pair I did
like and now I can't find it again.
Thirty minutes later I am thinking,
perhaps I ought to be buying grey trousers.

So I go to Starbucks
and have a large latte and a chocolate brownie.
Bad move.
I am now hyped up on sugar and caffeine
and I am probably not a size fourteen anymore.
Who cares. I rush round all the shops
trying on every pair of black trousers.
But in Wallis they are too formal
and in Top Shop they are too young
and in Karen Millen nothing fits me.
And in Laura Ashley they are too mumsy.
And in Primark they are too cheap.
And in Monsoon I lose the plot
and wow, look, an embroidered red velvet dress,
which I will only ever wear once in the next ten years.
But I love it! I love it!

And that is why I don't have any black trousers.

YOU ARE THE ONE FOR ME

The moment you rolled up that joint
I could see you were a man of distinction,
on a bender. Hey, scruffy, so unrefined,
do you want to know what's going on in my mind?

You are the one for me.
When I looked into your greeny brown eyes,
and only men of genius have eyes like that,
I had a past life memory
where I was an Egyptian princess and you were my eunuch.
(It was a very close relationship we had
back in the second century BC)
and I 'd like it to be something like that again,
but slightly more sexual.
I have to be honest here,
I find you devastatingly attractive,
when I saw you, my heart went plop, my brain went ping
and there was an explosion in my knickers,
(leopard skin satin).
And if that ain't love I don't know what is!
Because you are the one for me.
OK I might not look my best at the moment.
I've had a hard time recently with all that whiskey
and it looks like I have the dress sense
of a Polish librarian.
But, I'm the same age as Madonna
with the body of Anne Widicombe,
Don't laugh, I bet she looks pretty kooky
in a baby doll nightie.
What's appearances got to do with it anyway?
It's souls we're talking about here.
Twin souls that have been reunited
after several lifetimes of abstinence.
It wouldn't matter if I were a nine-year-old girl
and you were an octogenarian,
In fact you remind me of my great uncle Herbert.

Because you are the one for me,
My character could compliment yours entirely.
I've done my homework, I checked out your birth date.
I know that Pisces and Aquarius aren't usually compatible,
but we could make exceptions.
I mean, we are both visionaries,
and so what if your Pluto squares my Mars
and my Saturn does something nasty to your sun
who wants a dull relationship anyway?

The love I offer you is permanent.
It's more permanent than scar tissue,
more devastating than hurricane Katrina,
and more solid than a block of concrete
hurled out of a six-floor window.
Can't you feel it?
Can't you feel it?
Coursing through your veins
like intravenous chocolate pudding.

You are the one for me.
I'd do anything to make this work,
I want your babies.
I want all your babies, even the ones you've already got.
In fact, I could be your mother.
I can wake at half past four in the morning
and cook you green eggs and ham or spam fritters.
I can do the nurturing thing.
I can sing you Van Morrison songs in the bath.

Or we could be like cosmic brother and sister,
Isis and Osiris, and I know he lost his penis,
but hey, that was just a story,
and Isis is my goddess or is it Kali? I get confused,
but I'm in contact with the energy of all the goddesses,
because you are the one for me.

Don't walk away.
Can't you see you're missing a great opportunity?
A one way ticket to planet bliss
where we could live in... bliss forever for all eternity.
Stop running!
Just because I haven't had a relationship
in the last ten years,
doesn't mean I'm desperate. I'm just selective.
Come back! I'll give you everything,
a share of my mortgage, my wide screen television,
my Persian cat, my Persian carpet,
and my fourteen year old daughter
to try out first!

Come back! Come back!

You bastard!

SAFE

I'm not safe.
This body is too soft, too unprotected
from glass and knives and tainted cheese.
Car crashes, slippery steps.
Hepatitis, Weil's Disease.
Aeroplanes embedded in tower blocks.
Lightening strikes. Electric shocks.
Poisoned water. Poisoned blood.
Angry lovers. Dogs and floods.

Safe as houses.
They're not safe.
Toppling as the fault line splits.
The back door lets the burglars in.
The lighted gas blows all to bits.

But I feel safe.
Falling asleep next to you.
Our bodies touching like touching spoons
nestling in the kitchen drawer.

And spoons are safe.
And so is soup, and cake,
and hot chocolate at my Auntie's house.

And I remember safe.
At night in my Daddy's car.
Being driven home though rainy streets.
Past the rows of lit up shops.
The colours blurring in the wet.
It didn't matter if I fell asleep.
The windscreen wipers sweeping shush.
The headlights blurring in the wet.
The raindrops racing down the glass.
There was no heavy traffic, danger
or the day my dad would die.
There was me in my party frock and patent shoes.

My Daddy driving through the rain.
It didn't matter if I fell asleep.
When I woke up
I would be home.

SEA WALLS

Late summer. And I shall go to Sea Walls
down the avenue of chestnut trees
where the leaves are turning yellow
and have already begun to fall.

Sea Walls? The sea will never rise as high as here.
The cliff face. The rock edge.
The end of the city garden's playground.
And we shall sit on the bench by the ice cream van
and let our thoughts hang
like the climbers on the red ropes,
poised for a moment looking down
at the muddy river flowing towards the cranes of Avonmouth.
And in the distance the silver waters of the Severn
and the clouds on the black hills in Wales.

I was eighteen once. Beautiful and proud.
My first summer in an empty town.
In my old jeans, a lacy shirt and a hat with a flower,
I strolled every day across the downs
smiling like it was my own garden.

Three little white haired boys
playing with a kite.
It won't go up! It won't go up! And then it does.
They stand and watch it soar.
Three faces wide with wonder
at the shape of red disappearing into the blue.

I loved you once.
We loved each other with a passion that was quiet and real.
We tumbled out of bed from your Redland flat
and somehow made it across the downs
for breakfast in the Primrose café.
We sat there. Silent. Bombed out on sex
and love and love and love.
We had it so bad we could barely eat
our scrambled eggs.

Come with me now to Sea Walls
down the avenue of chestnut trees.
Where the leaves are turning yellow
and have already begun to fall.

Where the young men play football,
and the young girls stroll their heads held high.
They have never tasted sorrow.
Where the lovers are making promises they cannot keep.
And the little children run with kites
and their parents will remember
far beyond tomorrow.

THIS POEM

This poem is six years old.
Not finished.
Written in wobbly letters.
I like trees and the sun.
Eating apples in the orchard.
Grass stains on my shorts.
I can climb the highest branches.
Touch the clouds with dirty fingers.

This poem is fifteen.
Sulky.
Written in purple pencil
in an exercise book kept inside a shoe box,
inside another box,
at the back of the wardrobe.
Despairingly full of torment.
It's not fair. I have fat metaphors
and non-existent form.
I'm horribly, hideously, twistedly
overwritten. Oh, so much pain!

This poem is thirty-five.
Mature.
An elegant sweep with a gilded pen.
An invitation to adultery.
I'll meet you in the car park at Waitrose.
It's all style and Carol Ann Duffy.
The strangest thing I ever stole was your ideas.

This poem is ancient.
Trotted out at picnics and weddings.
Still funny enough to make us smile.
Still poignant enough to make us hold back tears.
Oh, yes we know this one.
"So long as men can breathe or eyes can see
so long lives this, and this gives life to thee."

This poem is just born.
A high pitched wail
Of a wet idea.

ANOTHER LIFE

I know you are happy
Ironing your shirts for work.
You'll be an Area Manager.
But when you are stuck in the queue
coming off the interchange,
breathing in the traffic fumes,
the Goddess will whisper in your ear.
There is another life.

Remember how you used to walk
in the April sun up Sugar Loaf.
Gasping to catch the air.
The hills and valleys all different greens.
A wisp of cloud like Skirrid's hair.
There is another life.

I know you are happy
buying toasters, curtains, kitchen tiles.
You fill your spare time with décor ideas.
But one Saturday at the Ikea till
thinking, is that lampshade the right shade of blue?
The Goddess will whisper in your ear.
There is another life.

Remember how you used to stand
in silence by the river Frome.
Watching the water flow and curl
in a shiny roar along the weir.
You threw a twig into the pull
and watched it sink and watched it stir.
There is another life.

I know you are happy
singing a nursery song to your baby son,
thinking all life begins from here.
But one night when you cannot sleep
and the silence creeps like a hungry cat.

You feel the weight you cannot feed.
You're not unhappy, no you feel fine,
but you used to play your guitar at night.
You haven't made a song for years.
The Goddess will whisper in your ear.
There is another life.

LET ME BE

Let me be. Let me be. Let me be...
your slut.
You know, the one you ring up
when you've had a row with your girlfriend.
And there she is. In a top that's too tight
and a skirt that's too short. And bare legs.
And you can have her. You can have her.
You can have her in the hall,
and on the stairs and in the bathroom and on the bog.
You can have her anywhere.

Let me be. Let me be. Let me be…
your drunk slut.
You know, the one that's been hanging
around the bar all evening with that hungry look on her face.
And now it's closing time
and you're the last decent cock that still works.
And here she comes.
A bit old and faded. Here she comes. A bit unsteady.
But you don't care, you don't care, you don't care

because you've had eight pints of Otterhead
to cloud your judgement
and besides, you're up for it.
So you ask her home, but you don't actually get there.
You land up in an alleyway
that smells of cider and piss and elderflowers.
And there you are shagging her against a fence
in a tangle of pulled down pants and trousers.
And when you do get home
you fall asleep straight away in a chair
and you don't hear her flitting about your house
like a trapped bird.

Let me be. Let me be. Let me be…
your mad drunk slut.
You know, the one who rings you up
twenty times a day even when you're at work.
You know, the one who sends you six love letters a week,
then runs screaming after you because she saw you
going into a shop with another woman.
You know, the one who's always hiding
behind that bush in your front garden
so when you leave your house
you're never quite sure whether she's there or not.
You know, the one who's always
peering in through your windows
and where did you leave your binoculars?
You know, the one who's so good at disguises
you're never quite sure whether
she's that old lady walking her dog,
or she's that man with a beard on the bus.
You know, the one who stands
outside your door for an hour in the rain
Until you let her in. Until you let her in.

Just so that you can talk to her.
Just so that you can say to her, "Please. Leave. Me. Alone."

But somehow it never gets to that.
Somehow it's always the same.
It's you on the sofa with your pants down
and one thought going through your head.
Oh, no. Oh, no. Oh yes…

Let me be. Let me be. Let me be…
your evil, mad, drunk slut.
Because she's so mad she knows exactly what she's doing.
She's getting through to you.
She's getting through to you.
She's becoming you.
She is you.

And you cannot extinguish her.
You cannot extinguish her no matter how hard you thrust.
Like the moth that flies into the candle again and again.
Ftt. Ftt. Ftt.
Fizzling with desire as you burn in the flame
of your crafty, evil, mad, drunk slut.

Your angel.

FROST AT MIDNIGHT

Full moon in December
and the landscape's turned an eerie white.
We're driving home across the Mendips.
There's no one here. A few sheep and us.
Warm in the car and overfed
on yet another pub turkey dinner.
No more Christmas parties please,
I may be a misfit but at least I'm not a total bore
like your boss.
Up the gear to sixty five.
If we start to slide I mustn't scream, you said.
Give me a man with a slow hand, sings the radio.
I need a man with a gentle touch.
The hedges zap by.
Not one who comes and goes in a sudden rush.
The wheels don't touch the road.
And we're flying. The moon's silver.
The trees are white. The road is a straight journey
towards the city which burns orange ahead of us.
In a few hours we will be asleep.
I want a different ending. Don't stop.
Let's keep driving through the night
through the frost and the lonely fields.
Where will we be by the morning?

SPRING FEVER

There's something in the air.
Does that mean things are going to change?
War is going to stop
and we'll be saying, "After you, how kind.
Would you like a cup of tea, Mr Al-Qaida?
The weather's getting better."
And here in Gritty Brit land
where everybody's grumbling,
"No more pointless wars and not another Tescos!"
We'll all start growing turnips and everlasting spinach.
We'll all skip together wearing hand woven natural fibres.

There's something in the air.
Does that mean things are going to change?
Perhaps another Jesus?
We'll walk about in sandals making miracles.
But then we would get locked up for causing public unrest.
And angels could rescue us and the police would fall down
and shout, "We have seen the glory of the Lord
greater than a neutron bomb!"

There's something in the air.
I thought I saw it.
A fuzzy bit of hope. A wet painting blurry star.
But perhaps it was Venus or the police helicopter
and I couldn't see straight because my eyes were tearful.

The cherry blossom's out now and the daffodils are laughing
on all the city roundabouts bursting out of winter.
And I'm wishing and I'm wishing
that things have got to change.

Things have got to change for young men at night
who want to be courageous?
They hug themselves for comfort
but their comrades' blood on their fingers
reminds them they're alone.

Things have got to change for women at night
who don't want to be courageous
but they hoped they might be.
Are thinking of young men.
Are thinking of lost children.
Who were never innocent
but they hoped they might be.
Are touching without talking.
Are walking without walking.
Through each other. Through each other.
Because they are empty. Because they are alone.

And things have got to change.
For potatoes in my cupboard have already starting sprouting.
Who told them that it's Spring?
Who told them as they sat there,
bald, fat potatoes?
Why can't I feel it? Are they more sensitive than me?

There's something in the air.
Why can't I feel it?
There's something in the air
And I want it to tell me that things are going to change.

A MUM CALLED MUM

I don't have a name. I am a mum called mum.

It starts early in the morning.
Mum! Where's my socks?
Mum! Me want dink.
Mum! I am doing jungles today and I have to wear green.
Mum! I can't find any green.

It continues right through the day.
Mum! Me want bik bik.
Mum! He won't give me my red car back.
Mum! I didn't want baked beans on the toast.
I wanted baked beans off the toast.
Mum! Me want more bik bik.

It's a noise. It varies.
Mum! (an angry shout)
Mum! (a cry of pain)
Mum! (a command for attention)
And that awful bored whine,
Muuuummmmmm.

Sometimes I just don't understand.
Mum! Me wanty frou frou.
Mum! What's the French for curtains?
Mum! Why are tables tables?

And sometimes I don't want to understand.
Mum! Ick. Mum! Poo. Mum! Ick poo.
Mum! Can Guinea pigs swim…?
Mum! If something stops breathing is that bad?

Sometimes it's heartbreaking.
Mum! Daddy's girlfriend is young and pretty.
Mum! Your tummy is all wobbly.
Mum! I want my Dad.
Mum! Why did Grandpa have to die?

And when they get older it's just more complicated.
Mum! I'm off to Australia. Bye!
Mum! Fuck Education. I'm going to live in a Eco Camp.
Mum! What happens when you take Acid?
Mum! Tables. Wow.
Mum! How do you know if someone is pregnant?

Then they leave and it's wonderful. It's so quiet.
I can sit in the garden and write poems and eat chocolate.
Meet my friends in cafés and read books on roses.
And have a job and have money and buy things like handbags and
go to Barcelona and wear gold sandals.

Then it all starts up again.
Grandma!

THE GOOD MORNING

I wonder what you and I did before we met?
Were we just babies sucking on a plastic cup?
Or little piggies snorting in a pen?
Happy slopping round in muck.
I think we were. Not quite human. Not quite grown up.
If anything I wanted. I got it. And you did too.
All pleasures satisfied.
Was that a way to live a life?

What did I do before we met?
I did a lot of shopping. I bought a lot of shoes.
Every lunchtime I choose a sandwich
from the *Tesco's Finest* range.
I met my friends at Mud Dock. I drank mocha. I ate cake.
I had my job, my house, my kids,
my garden, and believe me that was a special relationship.
Gardens are so temperamental
and they answer back with slugs.
I woke. I worked. I slept. I woke.

And what did you do before we met?
Just how much telly can one man watch?
When I met you I had never heard of Claude Van Damme.
I thought Martial Arts were decorations on a sword.
And how many junk rooms does one man need?
"That room's for your bicycles. That one's for your tools.
And that's the junk room. I see. I understand."
You had your ex-wives. All of them. Your sons.
You woke. You worked. You slept. You woke.

Now, last week did I hear you say,
"We must incorporate all the basic principles of design
into the garden plan?"
I thought you thought a garden
was a place to put your motor bike.
You were up a ladder brush in hand.
"Of course I much prefer

a terracotta maroony sort of red."
(This is from a man whose sofa was a foam filled sack).
And did I say, "Look, here's a Claude Van Damme film
I haven't seen"?
Whilst I explored the wonders of FNX or Sky Sports Two.
I never understood how Cricket worked and now I do.
We do Tai Chi together. A bit wobbly on my part.
You sit through Poetry gigs.
A bit confused. A bit amused. But that is Art.

So let us say Good Morning to our waking souls
And Good Night, Bye Bye, to what we were.
Each other is the one thing we can't control.
And lack of that is something we no longer fear.
Captain Kirk finds new worlds beyond the sun.
So let us go boldly to where other men have gone,
and women, who find that two are also one.

HE'S NOT MY CHILD

He's not my child.
My children were the white-haired Aryan Race.
Gold skin, blue eyes, red shorts.
Boy tumbling on boy running down the garden.
This one does silent jumps across the sofa.
He watches me and his dad.
He has eye's as dark as a rabbit's.
Except rabbits don't want to shoot people with BB guns.
(He's not allowed to have guns).
He likes Harry Potter. He likes being read to.
He knows when I get a word wrong.
He likes to talk. God, he likes to talk. About guns.
(He's not allowed to have guns).
He likes stories. So I tell him stories
of when my children were naughty.
When Loki stole the sweets from the shop.
And Boris locked my mother in the kitchen.
And Dory called his teacher a stupid cow.
He watches me his eyes growing wider and wider.
He has eyes as dark as a cave.
When I look inside I don't understand what's there.
I don't know the history of that wide-eyed look.
I didn't hold him in my arms.
I didn't link him to my breast.
We are strangers on either side of one man, his dad.
We watch each other trying to understand
I'm not his mother.

She phones when he comes to stay.
To check he's not up too late.
To check he's not drinking Coke.
To check he's not watching PG films.
I must remember. He has to go to bed at eight o'clock.
He mustn't get too tired or too excited.
Or deplete his kidney yin
by playing too many computer games.

I met her once down the shops.
Long flowing hair, those same dark eyes, long flowing skirt.
A siren strapped to a rock.
She said, "Don't let his dad let him get too tired."
She pleaded, "Don't let his dad let him get too tired,
he's just a little boy."

Save. Save. Save my boy from big bad men.
Don't let him turn into his dad.
Don't let him drink his beer and burp,
and turn his head at pretty girls.
And drink his soup with a slurp.
And grow up.

Of course, I said.
He's not my child.
I watch him talk bikes with his dad.
The bits and bolts. The know how stuff of hunting men.
They play fight down the stairs.
Shoot plastic arrows at the wall.
They gather wood for the fire.
And watch it burn. And watch the sparks.
The rising sparks and dark dark eyes.
A flashback ten thousand years.

THE HEART OF BRISTOL

You know it makes sense only 40 pence.
At the heart of Bristol,
The Evening Post.
Mum tells of sex molester.
Ban French foods say residents.
Welcome home to our little Betty.
Is Lord Lucan really dead?

You know it makes sense only 40 pence.
At the heart of Bristol,
The Evening Post.
Shops facelift face delays.
Cancer patients face delays.
Bus delays angers residents.
Take a fresh look at *Gardiner Haskins*
Docks development controversy.
Tall ships last voyage.
Brownies scoop cash prize.

You know it makes sense only 40 pence
At the heart of Bristol,
The Evening Post.
No to homeless hostel say residents.
No to Gypsy site say residents.
No to handicapped hostel say residents.
Bigot slur denied say residents.
Man found dead.
Gran's dog bites tot.
Do you know someone who's getting married?

You know it makes sense only 40 pence.
At the heart of Bristol,
The Evening Post.
Mahogany display cabinet glass doors £70.
Pair dark brown curtains with lining £50.
Three piece suite plus pouffe. Pink floral. £200 bargain
Fun loving girl wants to meet man. Keynsham.

City lose at home.
Rover lose at home.
Dreaming of another cup run?
We'll get it right in the end.
You know it makes sense only 40 pence
At the heart of Bristol.
The Evening Post.

TALKING ABOUT NORWICH

It was a cold winter the year he left.
The house was cold, my bed was cold.
My heart was as cold as permafrost.
I had the comfort of my female friends.
They said, "Get out more. Phone up a man.
Ask him out. Have some fun."
I thought about this. Then I remembered John.
A man at a party two years ago. Brown eyes. A smile.
We chatted, flirted. No harm done.
We were both in relationships then.

So, I phoned him. I said, "Remember me?"
He said, "Well, yes, I do."
I said, "My boyfriend's left me. I need cheering up."
He said, "What can I do? A drink?"
I said, "No. How about a country walk?"
It was February and freezing cold.
He said, "A walk?"
And now I was feeling like a complete fool.
I said, "Just somewhere different.
Everywhere in town reminds me of him."
There was a pause. I imagined John working this one out.
She's mad. No, she's sad,
and bad and dangerous as sad and silly women are.
"You aren't the first. You are the fourth one
 on my list." I said.
That wasn't strictly true. I had a list of four.
Perhaps first was fourth.
He laughed. He said, "I don't mind being fourth."

We met on Sunday. Hew had two hours to spare.
We left the city and headed north
up near Wotton where the Cotswolds fall away along the edge.
A frosty day. The ground was hard.
The puddles cracked like glass.
The conversation had already frozen up.
"I'm not my usual self," I said.

"This bust up has got me down."
"I know," he sighed. "My girlfriend left last year.
I'll never love again like that."
The sheep nudged the icy grass.
My hands were cold. I hadn't brought my gloves or hat.
His nose was red.
I knew nothing of this man except he had a charming smile.
And a broken heart.
Like mine. I said, "Tell me about yourself, I mean, where you went
to school and rode a bike and all that stuff."
He said, "I lived in Norwich. That's where I grew up."
"Norwich? I went to uni there.
Nobody I know has ever been to Norwich!"

And then it was as if the sun had come out
and warmed us both.
Do you remember Elm Hill when they cut down the tree?
And did you ever see the bosses in the cloisters?"
Of course I did. I spent hours in there
cricking my neck looking at the ancient stones.

And in the market place buying mushy peas.
Getting drunk and singing up the Unthank Road.
Surely you remember that?
The empty houses down St. Benedict's street.
The charity shops.
The tacky cinema.
The bus station, which had to be the vilest place on earth.

We were laughing now.
"Do you still go back?" I said.
"My parents left when I was eighteen. I've been back once.
The best years of my life I had in Norwich."
"Not the best years. The carefree ones." I said.
We were in the middle of a field. Somewhere up near Wotton.
Two people with the memory of a place.
I wasn't cold. And he was smiling like he could.

"It's time to go," he said.
I knew there wouldn't be anymore.
This was enough. We didn't need to meet again.
"I've had a great day, thanks," I said.
"And thank you too," he said, "I'll drive you home."

We don't know what people mean to us.
We don't know how long we have.
Some people stay together twenty years. Sometimes ten.
Sometimes it's only four. Or a weekend.
And sometimes we only have two hours
talking about Norwich.

DRINKING STARBUCKS COFFEE CAUSES GLOBAL WARMING

To the Prime Minister of England

Dear Sir,

I am a respectable married woman and mother of forty five a bit like your wife, and I am writing to you about a matter of great importance what I discovered travelling on a train from London Paddington to Bristol Parkway, that is,

DRINKING STARBUCKS COFFEE CAUSES GLOBAL WARMING.

Let me explain. At Paddington station I drank a cup of Starbucks cappuccino which as you know are always very large. Then going to Bristol on the train I had to go five times to urinate which means to piss.

Which is a lot if you think about it and not normal at all.

Then I thought what about all the other people on the train who have drunk Starbucks and what about all the times they have to piss and that got me really thinking.

I mean, what about all the people in London. I mean they are drinking Starbucks all the time, aren't they?

Now, on a train the piss goes into a tank, but in offices and homes where does all that piss go to and that extra water needed to flush it all away?

Now, I'm not stupid, I have worked in retail for 20 years and now I am in footwear, and I got a C in my geography but that was a long time ago but I know what a rift valley looks like. And I know that all this extra water will after sewage plants land up in our rivers and seas and what will happen then?

It will be extra warm because of all that piss and then THE ICE CAPS WILL MELT. I know this because I saw that film with Dennis Quaid and it went on a bit and I didn't get that stuff about what they all ate when they were locked in the library but I learned one thing.

And that is, that if the ice caps melt then THE PUMP IN THE SEA WILL GET SWITCHED OFF and the world will freeze and we will all be TOO DEAD to turn it back on again.

Now, I don't want this to happen . Because if the world freezes then you and me and all the trees and plants will die. And that will be a great shame because I have a WILDLIFE GARDEN and it's taken me two years to make that. I care about the planet. I don't put out slugbait because of the hedgehogs and I'm always chasing cats away because they eat the birds. And I'm sure you have a garden and a family too that you don't want frozen.

This is SO IMPORTANT that I think you should send this letter immediately to all countries in the world and especially the president of America because that is where Starbucks comes from and I'm sure they drink loads of it over there.

I think that all the Starbucks should be shut down AT ONCE because their coffee is the worst that makes you piss.

I have started up an action group in my street and we already have six people, seven if you count Jenny Taylor's daughter Molly who is eight. We have made posters and stickers that say.

STOP DRINKING STARBUCKS AND SAVE THE WORLD.

I hope that you will join us in this campaign and together we can save the world from a frozen disaster before it is all too late.

THE ENGLISH TEACHER AT LUMB BANK

We walked towards the chimney. It was taller
and the valley longer than I remembered.
The mill was dark and the trees were darker.
The sky was slate, the mud was black,
and the leaves a dirty yellow.

I wanted to take them further downwards.
I wanted to take them closer to the water.
I wanted them to hold the breadth of the chimney,
and touch the shadows of this valley.
I wanted to lose them in the tree side.

But the girls said,
"Miss, our trainers are getting muddy."
"Is that a rat?"
"No, stupid, it's a squirrel."
The black cat twitched at the window.
and the robin on the rooftop
called us back to lessons and paper.

Then the valley was filled with brightness,
holding the dregs of shadow by the water.
I saw the sun, my eyes glazed with light.
The mill, the trees, all gone, only when I looked down
I saw the trampled leaves. Our footsteps on the path.

Each moment is so very different
and this place, wet and dark this morning
was now a ringing golden bowl.
The robin would sing here.
The windows of the mill shine back the sunlight.

I will remember how we watched the squirrel
climb the tallest beech tree. The water from the mill,
brown like tea, pouring over the boulders.
And Charlie said, "It's disgusting Miss!"
But it wasn't. Oh, it wasn't.

I HATED LIVERPOOOL

Liverpool I hate you. Cultural Capital of what, exactly?
Your buses smell of sick and your streets smell of drains.
If they give you a facelift will you get a new personality?
I hate your weasel-faced tattooed fathers.
I hate your weasel-faced tattooed mothers.
I hate your ASBO sons with bad haircuts.
I hate your chain-smoking pregnant daughters.
Diversity means two sorts of tracksuits.
I hate the way you say "Birkenhead".
I hate the way you think Wirral is posh.

Liverpool I hate you.
You are a workman on a fag break.
You shout "fucking posh beetch!" when I walk past.
Yes, I'm a posh bitch and I'm proud of it.
I don't glorify my working class roots,
Quite simply because I haven't got any.
Can't you feel my Middle Class rage
fuelled by organic vegetables and education?
Education. Education. Education.
Liverpool, you haven't got any.
Education or organic vegetables.

You insult me then chat me up
when your missus is shagging your neighbour,
and your kids are out torching cars,
and you're wacking pints with your mates.
You chat me up then nick my handbag.
Your wit is as large as your penis.
Believe me I don't want to be on the end of either.
And why do you bang on about John Lennon?
He left the damn place don't you remember?

Wacca Macca I hate you.
The only thing I like
is the view of the water
I can see when I'm leaving.

Dear Passenger,

Welcome on board our Cross Country service. Your train today is our 'reserve' train, and not the usual Voyager, and I apologise for any inconvenience this may cause you.

Cross Country has 78 Voyager trains but due to the recent derailments, repairs, vandalism and things being thrown at trains or left on the track, and general neglect, we now have one in service and in order to give us some flexibility, through our partners The English Meat Marketing Board and Scottish Railway we have had to substitute other rolling stock.

The train has four standard class coaches and a luggage van. The doors are externally locking 'steel doors' which will be secured by an external bolt by our customer service advisor prior to departure. If you are not familiar with these types of doors instructions are clearly placed on them, which I ask you to read for your safety. You will also notice that there are no seats or windows. This is due to the carriage previously being used as a transport vehicle for an abattoir. For your comfort sacking has been placed on the floor and there are ventilation slats in the roof. Smoking is not permitted anywhere on the train.

There is no 'shop' or 'galley' on this train and unlike a Voyager this older type of train has no power points or audio systems and I am sorry for any inconvenience this may cause you. We will, however, offer you a complimentary cup of water.

There are also no toilet facilities but we recommend all customers make full use of the hole by the door.

At a station stop, should you wish to depart, please bang loudly on the steel doors and our customer care advisor will unlock the door and assist you onto the platform. In case of an emergency a bolt cutter is provided.

This train is unable to run at the usual Voyager top speed of 125mph. Please add approximately 4 hours to your journey time.

I hope you enjoy travelling with us today.

I WANT TO BE A BITCH

I'm sick of being sweet and charming.
Uncomplaining, undemanding.
I want to tell it how it is.
I want to be a bitch.

I want to say to my best friend.
You look awful in that dress,
like a bag of potatoes with a ribbon tied round.
And you need to lose weight. About three stone.
And that husband of yours
is a pompous bore, and is having an affair
with your sister. (I promised not to say).
And she's pregnant and, by the way, your children,
are ugly and not too bright, and can you please
stop talking about them all the time. Alright?

And I want to say to my mum. Shut up.
Shut up talking about curtains, and that little bit of stuff
you found in the market will make a nice cushion,
and in the high street they've just opened up
a nice new boutique that sells *Jacques Verte*.
I do not care. And I do not care about Mrs Whatsit's
eldest daughter Clare, who did so well
and now she's married to a doctor.
Mum, can you please say something that's interesting,
like what do you think about global warming
and poverty in America?
And do you think you've got dementia?

And I want to say to my dad.
Stop giving me tomato plants. They always die.
And yes, I do know that if I took
the second turning off the B31106
I would get there twenty minutes earlier.
And no, I don't want a very useful book
on how to mend my fridge.
And yes, I do know how to download my photographs,
And dad, why have you not hugged me

since I first grew breasts?
And why don't you go and see a therapist?

And I want to say to my daughter.
Stop showing me your scribbly drawings.
You have no talent, none, whatsoever.
But that won't stop you getting into art school.
So why don't you go now and stop bothering me
with your latest "Do you think he fancies me.
I think he fancies my mate Lisa?"
Darling, can you please grow up. I mean you are nineteen.
Is there nothing in your brain but mobile phones
and celebrity must haves?
Please learn to live on what you earn
rather than buying handbags.
Why don't you go backpacking to Thailand or Goa?
Why don't you go anywhere but here?

And I want to say to my son. Hello? Hello?
Is anybody in there, apart from MP3's
and Tomb Raider level six?
Have you, like, forgotten, how to, like yeah,
have a conversation with somebody, like whatever.
And you smell. I mean really bad, like last month's cheese.
And can you look at me instead of at your feet,
and take that bloody woolly hat off, please.

And I want to say to my partner,
Just do it. Go and buy a Harley and black leathers
and work out your midlife crisis.
I know, I know, your job's a bore,
you're out of shape; you don't know where it's all going.
So why don't you fuck off to Bali
and find some twenty two year old
who's drugged up enough to want to sleep with you.
Go swimming naked in the sea.
Fry your brains with ecstasy.

And I want to look in the mirror and say to myself.
What the fuck are you doing?
What are you? A one woman cooking, cleaning,
washing, counselling machine?
What are you? Fabulous at fifty? I don't think so.
You're underpaid and overweight.
Has it really come to this?
The ten pounds you spent on a top
in TK Maxx to make you feel young?
And what's worse, you'll never wear it.
Why don't you just go down the station
and take the next train out?

Why don't you find out what you want?
Do all those things you said you would,
like learn Spanish, live in Prague, climb Scafell Pike.
Wear red trousers and a quirky hat.
Shout more. Tell it how it is.

I'm going to like being a bitch.

THE QUIET LIFE

My head was in a spin.
I didn't have the time to talk to friends or think.
I was tempted by the quiet life.

So, now I'm in a seaside hotel
in somewhere unfashionable.
With décor that doesn't go;
blue stripy curtains and rose patterned wallpaper.
Gilt mirrors, pink carpets, boudoir furniture.
It's all en-suite but the shower door creaks,
and the toilet leaks,
and there's a view of the oil refinery.

My hostess is Jean Henderson, 56, wiry, twitchy.
She has perfected that chirpy cheeriness,
"Oh, do come in and make yourself at home.
breakfast is served at eight."

I was tempted by the quiet life,
now there's nothing to do
except watch oil tankers glide up the sound.
"We're usually so busy at this time of year."
Or walk up the coast road
and watch net curtains shift in the sea view semis.
Or count the empty shops down the high street.
Tourist information. Closed today.
Or join the teenagers snogging at the bus stop.

And there's nothing to eat except in the Indian
with purple walls and an overflowing dustbin.
Or the kebab shop
but even the teenagers aren't drunk enough for that.
Or Jean's a la carte, "We do do vegetarian."

Here the seventies aren't even retro.
And the picture of the Monarch of the Glen
isn't even ironic.

And the famous faces down the hallway are long forgotten.
The Kenny marsh band. Mo Winters.
Helen Shapiro 1965. To Jeanie with love.

She tries so hard with her tea and coffee sachets.
The blue chair by the window, the bathmat
that matches the curtains not quite.
And her little handwritten notes.
Do not put anything solid down the toilet.
Please do not use the hairdryer
and the television at the same time.
If you have an emergency in the night
please ring the bell under the horse picture.

Is this an emergency?
I haven't spoken to anyone for four days,
except to Jean to say, "You know,
I do think it's brightening up a little."
The most exciting thing I did today was go to Tescos.

I was tempted by the quiet life.
and I think I'm getting used to it.
Every time I look the sea's a different shade of grey.
In the marina the masts on the boats are clanking.
Two pied wagtails fly over the jetty.
Jean's cooking her rump steak special.
The smell is wafting through my window.
Another tanker coming up the river.

CEMETERY ROAD

She picks him up from morning school.
"What shall we do today?"
"Let's go to Cemetery Road."
A treat for a six-year old. "And what shall we eat?"
"Pork pie, crisps and coke!"
It's the same every week.
They take the bus to the end of town
and buy their lunch in the garage shop.

Cemetery Road in Totterdown.
Past the school playground.
There's a red bicycle and a ginger cat.
A tub of daffodils. A bag of sand.
At the end is the wall and the iron gates.
There's a derelict house.
"We could live in there and paint it white."
"Do you think the dead people walk around at night?"

There's the grave of Arthur heap and beloved Maud
and the marble angel for the boy called George.
"How did he die?"
"I don't know, it was long ago."
The grass is waist high, the brambles twist.
They walk along the path to the white cross,
the war memorial for the glorious dead,
where they sit and eat their picnic lunch.

What shall we do today? Let's go to Cemetery Road.
Somewhere in my memory is a young mother
with old jeans and a faded coat,
and a child with blonde curls and scuffed down shoes.
For once he's not kicking at the world.
He's eating, pork pie, crisps and drinking coke.
Where the houses stop and the trees begin.
And the city has been left behind.
This is the wilderness. This is paradise.

HALF LIFE

Sunday six o'clock. I'm on the sofa watching Time Team.
An archaeologist in a rainbow jumper debates whether
the bones are Anglo Saxon or earlier.
And look, they've found another bit of pot.
It's raining. A blackbird's singing. Summer's over.
Another weekend's gone,
and you're upstairs playing Half Life.

When the kids left home I thought we would have
weekends in the Prescelis.
Walk up Carningli from Newport.
Look at the view to Wicklow.
Lean our backs on Pentre Ifan.

But you're upstairs playing Half Life
and I'm watching bones being dug out of the mud.
It's complicated. They use a tiny trowel and brush.
"Do we know yet? Are they male or female?"
I want to be there, in the mud,
on the slope of a hill-fort in the Marches.
I want to run down to the woodland.
I want to smell the bracken and the nettles.

"Do you want some supper?" I call upstairs.
"Yeah, what you making?" You call back.
Half a chicken. Tomatoes. Pasta.
Pieces I can put together.

When the kids left home I thought we would eat out more.
Try a new restaurant every week.
There's a Japanese one by the harbour.
There's a Lebanese one in Clifton.
But I'm on the sofa watching Time Team
and you're upstairs playing Half Life.

The skeleton hasn't got a head. "Which is strange,"
says the presenter. The reasons are discussed.
War. An accident. A beheading. A Saxon man without a head.
Buried next to him are a woman and a baby.
"These were tough times," says the presenter.
Upstairs you are killing Aliens.
They shriek and splat and disappear.

When the kids left home
I thought we would have more holidays.
I've never been to Prague or Moscow,
or Warsaw, or Ankara, or Helsinki,
or Reykjavik, or Dublin or Tbilisi.
You've never been to Paris.

A blackbird's singing in the pyracantha.
It's raining and it's getting darker.
A Saxon family have been slaughtered.
I haven't started on the salad.
And you're upstairs playing Half Life.

MY LIFE AS A PORN MOVIE

There I am lying on my bed in my lacy nothings fondling myself
when the door bell rings.
"Who can this be?" I exclaim and totter down stairs,
(I am wearing high heels).
And, look, it's my best friend Polly and she says,
"I've just been out buying sexy underwear,
so I thought I'd bring them round to show you."
"Oh, please come in," I simper and before you can say
is this realistic? We rush upstairs and start
peeling off our clothes.
"Oh Polly," I whisper, "red satin and black lace,
I would never choose anything so bold."
"And your underwear is so creamy and silky,"
she breathes, "it's so sensual to touch."
So, before you can say, do your friends have exactly the same bra
size as you? We start trying on each other's underwear.
"Oh Polly, wearing red satin makes me feel quite naughty," I tease.
"And I feel all virginal," she responds.
So we start fondling each other's breasts.

Cue naff soft rock music,
and we are rolling around on the bed.

Then there's a noise outside,
"Oh no it's the window cleaner," I shriek,
"I quite forgot he was coming."
So the window opens and the window cleaner falls in.
"I know what you ladies need," he guffaws
and starts to take off his boiler suit.
And before you can say, how come the window cleaner's
a handsome hulk and not a fat, hairy arsed oaf
like they usually are? He is naked and with an enormous,
"Oh my god!" I squeal.

Cue close up shots of erect penises, split beavers
Penetration. Penetration. And penetration.
And more rock music. This time a lot louder
And more rhythmical.

Oh, Ah, Oh, Ah, Oh, Ah,

Then the door bell rings. "Now who can this be?" I muse.
And before you can say, who wrote this plot line?
I open the door to the entire England football team.
"We heard there was a party round here," says David Beckham,
(who, as you know, is no longer in the England football team).

So they go upstairs. Meanwhile Polly and the window cleaner
have decided to watch my saucy downloads.
The football team crowd round.
"This is boring, have you got the last European cup final?"
says David…
and bizarrely I have.

Then the doorbell rings again. And before you can say
this porn movie is getting very strange. I totter downstairs.
And it's Monty Don! Of course, this isn't a porn movie anymore.
This is my private fantasy.
"Oh, Monty," I say talking normally now, "I am so glad you are
here, I'm having so much trouble with my garden. High terraces,
north facing, What can one do with such an aspect?"
"Well, I do like a challenge," says Monty.
So I put my gardening coat over my skimpies,
kick off my high heels and get my wellies on.
And we go and tackle the problem.

"Hmm, it's quite simple," says Monty.
"All you need is a complete
restructuring, a few stone walls and a water feature."

And because this is my private fantasy
this all happens in the next few seconds.

There we are drinking tea on the newly created outdoor
chill out area.
From the house are the shouts of the football team,
the window cleaner, and Polly.

But it all seems far away and my house isn't a two bedroomed
terrace anymore it's a mansion.
And it isn't in the city, it's in West Pembrokeshire.
And my garden isn't twenty foot long it goes on for acres.
"Let me show you the rest of it," I say to Monty.
So we wander through the sunken garden, the rose beds,
and past the herbaceous borders,
"Such original planting," says Monty,
through the prairie slopes and the woodland glade.
"You know, this is one of the most interesting gardens
I have ever seen," says Monty
admiring my collection of rare maples.

And finally the garden ends in a valley
sloping towards the sea.
We sit there surrounded by this landscape
of unparalleled natural beauty.

An exquisite moment better than any orgasm.

FALSE ALARM

4am at The Thistle hotel, Birmingham.
I am woken, for the second night, by the fire alarm.
I throw on nearest available clothes.
Jeans. Tee-shirt. No bra.
The noise deafens. We head for the stairs.

Last night, when this happened, we were excited.
"Do you think there really is a fire?"
"Or a bomb?"
"Oh look! Here comes the fire engines!"
We laughed at each other's choice of bed wear.
There is no humour now.

Our 4am attire is more random. Flip flops.
Dressing gowns. Pyjamas and coats.
Bare feet. Even the dude, who turned up last night
in a black suit and hat, is dishevelled.
Three shiny fire-engines arrive and a platoon of firemen.

No one speaks. The rain pours.
We huddle under the canopy in front of the lobby.
If there really were a bomb we would be ripped
to pieces. The firemen rush in. They are doing their job.
As is the receptionist who waves paper and shouts.

We wait. The alarm stops.
We wait. A baby cries.
The receptionist says, "I haff to call ze roll call"
and starts with the top floor. "601. 602. 603."
We answer limply. "Here." "Over here."

"621. 622. 623."
The receptionist looks about fifteen. He looks tired.
I wonder if he is Polish. Slovakian. Slovenian.
My room number is 456.
The firemen come back. There is no fire or bomb.

We knew this. "A comfortable night at the Thistle,"
the brochure said. I am cold.
I want to sleep. I realise
there is going to be more of this.
More bomb scares. More bag searches. More false alarms.

And all because? Then I see him by the lift.
Long beard. Pyjama suit. A Muslim!
And oh my god he's carrying a rucksack!
He's not a terrorist. He's with the wedding party.
The grandmas in headscarves. The old men with longer beards.
The babes in arms. Aunties, sisters, cousins.
And two young men cradling
their families' most treasured possessions:

the wedding flowers.

THE PASSIONATE ACCOUNTANT TO HIS LOVE

Come live with me and be my love
and then I will let you move
the coffee table and bookcase
to make a better use of space.

I'll bin the carpet. Sand the floor.
(You have a good eye for décor.)
I'll like the curtains you will choose.
Geranium reds? Delphinium blues,

With a contrasting splash of pink?
We'll buy a brand new kitchen sink
and worktops in eco beech.
Oh, happiness is within our reach!

I'll throw away my railway mags
and collection of hoover bags.
And the cushions made by Auntie Rose,
I understand you don't want those.

I'll throw away my computer stuff,
for one PC is quite enough.
I don't need five. I know you're right,
they block the hallway's natural light.

Come live with me and be my love
and I will my commitment prove
by taking you to Ikea
more than twenty times a year.

We'll buy a 'Strib' stripey rug,
an 'Aardik' lamp, a hand blown jug,
and because you say my sheets smell
we'll get a duvet set as well.

I'll transform my bachelor mess
and then your friends will be impressed.

TEMPLE CLOUD

I don't think about you much.
But the bus stopped in Temple Cloud.
The bus to Wells. Leaving the city for the countryside.
Temple Cloud. A street of houses.
Two pubs and the fields behind,
ploughed. It was November. A few leaves left.

Twelve years ago you were twenty eight.
I was a single mum with no money
and not much hope.
You drove lorries, but you weren't a lorry driver,
you said. No, you were the tribe of one.
A traveller in your own head.

You lived in one room in Totterdown.
And you had a stammer, and it was bad.
You coughed and wiggled and shook
to get the words out. A strange dance.
Blue eyes, ruffled hair, a slip of a man
with big hands.

When the children were asleep I crept down to you.
You made me soup and we drank it in bed in cups.
We watched "Dad's Army" and the late night films.
You didn't sleep.
You never slept. You sang me John Martyn songs.

And I told you my dreams. A tree on an island in a lake.
A temple in the desert. A cloud that sang.
You said, "You're the best thing."
I said, "You're bonkers." And you were.
You smoked dope for Breakfast. Dropped acid for lunch.
Drove like a maniac. Danced like a madman. Hated schedules.

That Christmas, when the children went to their Dad's,
we went to Solihull. Your mum invited us.
The car broke down. We turned up well past midnight.

Your family were still up. Sitting there
arms folded. You've let us down again.
And it went on for four days.

You sister contradicted everything you said.
Your other sister sulked. Your brother started
play fights that weren't play. Your mother said,
"So, when are you going to get a proper job?"
"And be respectable," said your dad.

You couldn't answer. You couldn't speak.
You shook and coughed and waved your hands.
We slept on the mattress in the dining room.
"Families are hell," I said, "but yours is worse."
You shook your head.
You loved them.

And now you live in Temple Cloud.
In that sixties bungalow?
Or in those stone cottages by the road?
And what do you do in Temple Cloud?
Do you still drive lorries? Your girlfriend doesn't work.
I heard she had a breakdown and you look after her.

What do you do in Temple Cloud?
Do you go down the pub? Do you walk up the lanes?
Do you still sing John Martyn songs?

"May you never lay your head down,
without a hand to hold.
May you never make your bed out in the cold."

DEATH IN THE TRAVELODGE

I could be anywhere.
Same stale foot smell. Same blue check carpet.
Same blue check duvet.
And a window that doesn't open to the Leisure Park piazza.

Cambridge. Nandos, Subway, Starbucks,
Warner Brothers, Bowling Alley, Blockbuster.
Ring Road, Railway, Depot,
Self -Storage, New Build, Business Zone.

It's not the Cambridge I remember at nineteen.
Students on Kamikaze bicycles.
Chocolate cake in the Copper Kettle.
The silence on the Fellows' lawns.

I flick through digital channels.
Holby City. Sportsnight. Culture Show.
Poirrot. Midsummer Murders. Miss Marple.
Perhaps the cheeseburger and extra fries will do it.

I walked to Granchester on Sunday
listening to larks rise from wet grass.
And something about hawthorn blossom,
and willow trees and wet grass.
I can't remember who I was with,
but I wore a Laura Ashley dress,
pale red with pink flowers,
and we talked about Gerard Manley Hopkins.

Eamon lived in a turret
and his bedroom overlooked the market.
He brewed beer for the King's College parties.
Simon had a room in Gonville so damp his shoes went mouldy.
Paul, at St. John's, was a choral scholar.
He shared a panelled oak apartment with a lord.
And Nick, at Peterhouse, said he hated it,
he'd rather sell ice-cream to tourists.

I climbed over the wall in a silk gown,
at midnight, into Peterhouse gardens,
a bottle of champagne in my hand.
I wasn't even a bloody Cambridge student!
Smuggled in for parties and May Balls.
Dancing on the lawn in my high heels.
Crying in my torn dress in the morning.

THE EXPERIMENT

AIM

The experiment set out to prove that a man and woman cannot watch television on a Saturday night without arguing.

METHOD

1. A man and woman who had been living together for more than four years were used.

2. They were placed on an Ikea Extorp two seater sofa in front of a Phillips 28 inch widescreen television.

3. They were provided with two bottles of sauvignon blanc, eight cans of Fosters lager, two party size packs of Cheesy Doritos and a 250 gram tub of salsa dip, and thirty six digital channels with TV on demand functions.

THE EXPERIMENT

The experiment began at 8pm. British Summer Time.
The couple decided to watch 'Casualty'. No arguments were observed.
Units of alcohol drunk. None. Doritos consumed. None.

At 9pm the couple decided to watch a film using the film on demand function. There were four hundred options.

At 9.45pm they had decided on two options. Bridget Jones 2 and The Matrix 3.

The man said, "Bridget Jones. I can't stand that fat cow."

The woman said, "Oh for God's sake we'll watch The Matrix, then."

At 10.pm the woman said, "This is like the last two! It's pretentious, I mean the analogy between god and computers is so dated, and Nemo as a Christ figure, I mean can you believe it?"

The woman ate 90 grams of Doritos and drank two units of wine.

At 10.15 the woman said, "I am dying of boredom."

The man said, "That's it, you've spoiled it."

The woman said, "There must be something we both like." Her posture was observed as being seductive.

At 10.30 they had selected to watch "The Eternal Sunshine of the Spotless Mind"

By 10.40 four units of wine and two and half units of lager had been drunk and the woman had removed her jumper.

By 10.45 the man was asleep. The woman, who was transfixed by the film, ate the rest of the first packet of Doritos and all of the salsa dip.

At 11.12pm the man woke up. He said, "Oh look Kirsten Dunst in her knickers."

The woman said, "Shut up, this is interesting."

The man said, "Yeah, she might take her knickers off."

The woman said, "Shut up! It's so romantic. He's having his memory wiped because he's in love with her and he can't stand it."

The man said, "Huh, I know what he feels like. Mind you Kirsten Dunst is quite cute."

The woman shouted, "He's not in love with her, he's in love with Kate Winslet!"

The man said, "Not another fat cow!"

The woman screamed, "What is it with you and normal women? They are not fat they are just curvy and normal. Kirsten Dunst has got bones sticking out."

The man said, "Ha, Ha, so I have I. Ha Ha."

The woman threw an empty can of lager at him.

At 11.30pm the man said, "Why is her hair blue? Haven't we seen this bit before?"

The woman said, "It's postmodern you idiot. The story is going backwards."

The man said, "Wait a minute, isn't that the guy from Lord of the Rings."

The man drank two units of lager and said, "Where's that packet of Doritos?"

The woman said, "Shut up. I ate them."

The man said, "What all of them? And the dip? You pig."

The woman said, "Please shut up this is poignant."

The man said, "I can't believe you ate all those Doritos. You'll get fat like that Kate."

"She is not fat!" screamed the woman and threw the other packet of Doritos at him.

The man drank two more units of lager and the woman drank another unit of wine.

The man ate the whole of the second packet.

At 12.15 the film ended.

At 12.16 the man said, "God that was crap."

At 12.17 the woman said, "Do you really think I am fat?"

The man said, "Oh look, it's Tottenham."

The woman said. "I hate you."

The woman slammed the door. The man stretched out on the sofa and drank the remaining cans of lager.

At 12.30 he went to the kitchen and made himself a pickled onion and tomato paste sandwich. He went back to the sofa, ate the sandwich and drank the rest of the wine.

At 12.45 he found the adult channels.

At 2.00 am he was ready for bed. He ran up stairs, taking off his clothes, and bounced into bed saying, "Hmm, darling, you smell nice."

The woman rolled over and yelled, "What are you doing! Get off me! God you stink of pickled onions! Do you know what the time is?"

The man said, "I thought you were feeling romantic.

At 2.15am they were both asleep. The woman in the bed and the man on the sofa.

At 2.16am the experiment ended.

CONCLUSION.

The experiment was successful. It proves, without doubt, that it is impossible for a man and woman to watch television on a Saturday night without arguing.

FULL SUPPORT

In my over shoulder boulder holder,
and my midriff encased in elastic,
I can barely breathe, but I look fantastic.
I can't bend down or turn around, but do I really care?
I am feeling the benefits of full support underwear.
Listen to your girlfriends. Listen to Gok Wan.
You'll never Look Good Naked
without your elastic knickers on.

My elastic knickers on. My elastic knickers on.
I am a goddess with my elastic knickers on.

Girls, get busy. Sort out your knicker drawer.
Chuck out those itchy, scatchy, lacy things
that leave you feeling sore.
Chuck out those ugly boy pants.
Chuck out those twisted thongs.
And feel the support you've never had
with your elastic knickers on.

My elastic knickers on. My elastic knickers on.
It feels like I'm being hugged by my best friend
with my elastic knickers on.

Forget size skinny zero. Forget a perfect ten.
It's a firm and curvy sixteen
that will get you all the men.
And all the women too, if you can wait that long.
Every one will fancy you with your elastic knickers on.

My elastic knickers on. My elastic knickers on.
I'm just so damn munchy with my elastic knickers on.

My boyfriend gets jealous. He thinks I'll bump into my ex.
But I say "Darling, be realistic,
in these things you can't have sex.
It takes an hour to peel them off and an hour to squeeze them on.

Darling, I'll be faithful to you,
with my elastic knickers on."

My elastic knickers on. My elastic knickers on.
I'm a fricking vestal virgin with my elastic knickers on.

So come on girls let's muster
on England's pastures green.
Was not the Holy Lamb of God in elastic knickers seen?
I will not cease from mental strife,
nor shall the sword sleep in my hand.
'Til I have brought elastic knickers
to England's green and pleasant land.

Yes! The saints and apostles and the whole almighty throng
will welcome me to heaven with my elastic knickers on!

APRIL IS THE CRUELLEST MONTH

I hate April. Where's the sodding rain
and the lilacs have been breeding in my garden.
The German students mumble things.
"Ve used to go sledging in ze snow
but now zis global warming.
Och die schlete Welt. Ich Vermisse meine Heimaten"

The ground's too hard to dig. Dandelion roots
in the stony rubbish.
The hyacinths have come out white not blue.
The bonkers witch next door is doing the Tarot cards
with her one eyed dope dealer husband.
"Oh beware the hanged man."
(He's got his string vest on).
Unreal inner city in an April heatwave.
The bird the cat killed is sprouting in my garden.

And all you want to do is play chess.
The plastic chair I sit in,
given to us by your mother, is no throne.
We need a new patio table. One that doesn't wobble.
Whoops there goes my king. My bishop took your pawn.
Your pawn is near my queen.
My nerves are bad today. The sun hurts my eyes.
Let's go down the pub
and talk to toothless Lil, who hates students,
especially Germans.

Fortunately they are asleep after last night's party.
The rubbish piled high, cans and bottles and other things
the cat will bring into our kitchen. Like the rat he found
last week and the thrush I tried to bury.
Oh no, they're awake
and have started playing their guitars.
Weila la la la la la.
Weila la la la la la.

One eyed Tiresias looks more perky.
Perhaps the students will start sunbathing,
especially the cute blonde one, Nina,
I'm sure he spies on her in the shower.
Perhaps I should warn her. I'll do it later.
Weila la la la la la
Weila la la la la la

I wish it would rain. Buckets of the stuff.
Wash the streets clean.
Wash the cat shit off the path.
Wash the fag ends off the patio.
Wash the witch out to sea.
Wash the students back to Berlin.
Weila la la la la la
Weila la la la la la

Did I just hear thunder? Perhaps it was a plane.
There's a cheap flight to Berlin.
I will remind the students.
What was that sound high in the air?
Hopefully it was thunder.
God, I want some rain.
The witch has started chanting.
Datta. Dayadhvam. Damyata.
We've all gone mad.
Check mate. I lost the game.

DONTCHA

I'm on a mission to liberate mums.
Forget your fretting and have some fun.
No more farmers' markets and organic food
and buying houses next to the best schools.

And if you won't listen, I'll ask the kids.
I know they want it. A mama who's fit.

Don't ya wish ya mama was hot like me.
You won't be swot with a mama like me.
Dontcha. Dontcha.
Don't ya wish ya mama was a freak like me.
You won't be a geek with a mama like me.
Dontcha. Dontcha.

No more SATS tests and GCSE's.
You don't need them. Because the party is free.
I'll seduce your teacher and get you off school
and we'll go shopping, because shopping is cool.

Don't you wish your mama was hot like me.
You won't be a swot with a mama like me.
Dontcha. Dontcha.
Don't you wish your mama was a freak like me.
You won't be a geek with a mama like me.
Dontcha. Dontcha.

I won't tell you to turn your music down.
I can't hear it, because I've got my own.
I won't tell you I've had enough.
But I'll tell you that your mates is buff.
Stop your fretting. Leave it alone.
Because if you can't party, it ain't a happy home.

Don't you wish your mama was hot like me.
You won't be a swot with a mama like me.
Dontcha. Dontcha.
Don't you wish your mama was rich like me.
Don't you wish your mama was a bitch like me.
Don't you wish your mama was cool like me.
Don't you wish your mama was a fool like me.
Dontcha. Dontcha.

I WAS BORN IN A STRANGE COUNTRY

I was born in a strange country
of red dry earth and heat all year
and the sweat ran down my back.
And elephants worked in the logging camps.
Where coconuts grew by the beaches
and the sun was so hot we sat in the shade.
Where the village women brushed their babies' hair
and wore saris as bright as paradise birds.
And my mother drank tea in the Mount Lavinia Hotel
and my nanny told me stories of Krishna,
which she didn't learn from the convent,
where the little brown girls in white dresses
walked in an orderly line.
I was born in a strange country
where the villagers wailed when somebody died
and the radios wailed through the afternoon
and the diesel train wailed in the cutting.
Where high in the hills in the tea plantations
the tea pickers' fingers never stopped clicking.
And in the temple at Kandy
the Buddha's tooth was in a golden shrine.

I was born in a strange country
with trees that never stopped fruiting
in the Hakgala gardens and Nuwara Eliya
flowers were as big as my face
and bougainvillea trailed over the walls.
But the houseboy killed a snake in the bathroom
and my mother went swimming in the beach club.
(Whites only, no natives allowed).
And my nanny brushed her hair with coconut oil
and told me stories of Kali,
her necklace of children's skulls
and her terrible, enticing smile.

I was born in a strange country
where my mother dressed for the races,
and my father cursed the servants
because they were never on time.
But the servants bowed and nodded and smiled
they didn't care at all that nothing was ever on time.
And the cook would only make custard
(so we ate a lot of custard)
and my brother tripped on the veranda
and cut off half his finger
and my nanny spooned me eau de cologne,
(two bottles she stole from my mother)
and scented and drunk I lay in my cot
and watched the electric fan.

I was born in a strange country
with beaches too hot to walk on
and waves too fierce for swimming
and beggars outside the churches.
Crumbling Portuguese buildings.
and white bony cows walked through the market
And theTamils hated the Sinhalese
and there was a curfew at nine.

I was born in a strange country.
A country that did me no good.
A country that nearly killed me.
But even now things seem unfamiliar
that should be so familiar.
Like tweedy jackets and vicar's wives.
Like pac-a-macs and wellies.
Red pillar boxes and buses.
Umbrellas, crumpets and marmite.

Because I was born in a strange country.
And I hate the cold and the dark and the wet long winters
and I lie in my bed at night and I hear the swish of a fan.

FAMILY PRAYERS

God bless Mama, and God bless Dada,
And God bless Toby, Lucy, Mary, Emily and Katy
and make them good.

Hail Mary full of grace.
The Lord is with thee.
Blessed art thou amongst women and blessed is the fruit
of thy womb, Jesus.

"What's a womb?"
"Shh, Mary, we'll tell you later.
Put your hands together, and close your eyes
and pray.
Look. Lucy's doing it properly."
Yes, I'm doing it properly
because this is family prayers
and I'm praying for us all to be good.

God bless Toby and make him a good boy and pass his exams.
God bless Lucy and make her nearly as clever as Toby
God bless Mary and make her do her singing practice.
God bless Emily and may her reading get better.
And God bless Katy and may she grow up properly
because there's something slightly wrong with her.

Our Father who art in Heaven.
Hallowed be thy name.
Thy will be done.
Thy Kingdom come on earth as it is in Heaven.

My father, sitting on the bed.
Not kneeling on the floor like the rest of us
because he has a bad knee.
His voice booming straight up to God.
"Forgive us our trespasses!"
"What's a trespasses?"
"Shh, Mary, we'll tell you later.
Put your hands together and close your eyes

and pray.
Look. Lucy's doing it properly."
Yes, I'm doing it properly.
I'm kneeling on the floor
in my pyjamas, dressing gown and slippers.
There's that smell of shampoo, talcum powder,
warm baby milk and hot water bottles.
Katy, in her cot, is nearly asleep now.
My mother is still wearing her apron.
My red dressing gown has little buttons like ladybirds.
Even when I close my eyes I can feel them.

I'm praying.
God bless Toby and make him pass his exams.
God bless me and may I get a bike for Christmas.
I don't think I'm supposed to ask for that.
God bless Mary and I hope
she gets bubonic plague and I hate her.
I don't think I'm supposed to ask for that either...

Hail holy Queen, mother of mercy.
Hail our life, our sweetness and our hope.
To thee do we cry poor banished children of eve.
Mourning and weeping in this vale of tears.

I'm praying
because we are the poor banished children of Eve,
banished to Katy's bedroom to pray every night.
I'm praying for wars to stop.
I'm praying for the starving babies in Africa.
I'm praying for Grandpa to get better.
I'm praying for us all to be good.
I'm praying so hard
that if I close my eyes tighter surely I can feel
my own guardian angel standing right behind me.
And surely, surely I can feel the faint rustle
of his huge resting rainbow wings.

Family prayers. Every night before bedtime.
Even when I was fifteen. Even when I was sixteen.

God bless Mama and God bless Dada.
God bless Toby and make him pass his exams.
God bless Lucy and make her a good girl
especially now she's got a boyfriend.
God bless Mary and stop her wearing make up to school.
God bless Emily and may her reading get better.
God bless Katy and let's hope she learns to talk.

And God bless Uncle Stan, and Auntie Topsy
and Auntie Blanche and Uncle Ron,
and Uncle Will and Alfred George and Mrs Basset
and Tommy and Mr Kavachovitch.
And may they rest in peace.
And God bless
Grandpa and Grandma and the other Grandma
and John Dodsworth who was only fifteen.
And Auntie Jo.
And Dada.
And Sonia's baby.
And may they rest in peace.

Eternal rest give unto them Oh Lord
And let perpetual light shine upon them.
And may they rest in peace.
Amen.

MY MOTHER AND MY SISTER

PART ONE.

They're standing at the window. My mother and my sister.
My mother a bit bent now and peering hard.
She can't see too clearly.
And Katy, hanging on my mother's arm.
She's half a head smaller.
She sees me first. She calls out.
"Here she is. Here she is. Here's my big sister!"

She was the last child. I knew all about babies.
How they cried at night, and sucked bottles,
and how to put a nappy on.
I was ten. Babies didn't interest me much.
My mother brought her home. A little thing.
With dark hair and a screwed up face.
She didn't cry. She lay in her cot and slept.
And slept. My mother woke her up to feed her.
This wasn't right. Babies screamed and kicked
and punched the air with tiny fists.
She slept. If I put my finger near her hand
she sort of held it.
My mother was tired. Bedraggled in a dressing gown.
She slept too.
My father said we had to be very quiet. Shh.
There were no parties. No people coming round.
No vases of flowers.
Just silence in our house and snow outside.
The tracks of a cat across the white.

My mother called us upstairs. She had lipstick on.
Like she did when she was going out.
The bedroom smelled of zinc baby cream.
And *Coty L'aimant*, eau de toilette.
My sister in the wicker cot. Asleep as she always was.
"I have something you tell you," said my mum,
"about your sister."

Katy was on her front, her arms spread out
like a floppy doll.
My mother coughed and smoothed down her skirt.
My dad held her hand. "There's something wrong.
She won't grow up."
Well, that's what I heard. Be a baby always?
Why was that so bad?
My mum went on, "She won't do things like she should."
My father said , " ... will need extra help...
there's name for it,
Mongoloid."

I listened now. Mongol. Mongol. I knew what that meant.
There was one on the bus. "Oi Mongol boy!"
He dribbled when he smiled.
He smelled of pee. He shuffled when he walked.
I mustn't touch him or I'd get it too.
Mongol. Idiot. Stupid. Daft. Not quite there. My sister?
Dark fluffy hair. A squashed up face. Chinese eyes.
My brother cried. "None of that," said my mum.
"There's no time for that." She sat up very straight,
"The doctor said,"
she raised her voice, like she did when she told us off,
"the doctor said, put her in a home,
but I won't consider it."
Nobody talked back to Mum when she was cross.
Not my Dad or even Doctors.
"We won't ever, ever, put her in a home."

PART TWO

My sister. The ugly cabbage patch girl.
Who took two years to walk and when she did
we had to stop her running.
Who giggled when she got told off.
Whose first words were, "Me too!"
Who had no fear about the dark, or spiders.
Who went up to people in the street
and said, "Hello, who are you? I like dogs."
Who could do jigsaws better than me.
Even those thousand piece ones of sea and sky.
I mean, Katy, how do you know that piece is right?
"I just do."

My sister. Who liked to spin like Wonderwoman.
Who learnt to knit and made scarves two feet long.
Who liked matches far too much
and set alight anything she could.
Including my auntie's kitchen.
My sister who my mother taught to sit up straight.
Who my mother taught to say, "Nice to meet you,
thank you so much. I like cake."
Who my mother taught to read.
Despite the Doctors saying she wouldn't.
My sister who could read because for three years
everything in the house was labelled.

My mornings were like this:
Get up, get dressed and go the kitchen,
(labelled 'Kitchen door').
Open door with handle ('Handle').
Go to fridge (labelled, 'Fridge') and take out
pint of milk (with a little label on it 'Milk').
Find bowl in cupboard ('China cupboard') and also cup.
Make tea in teapot (with a tea stained label 'teapot').

Even now when I open a cupboard door
I half expect to find labels.

Marmalade. Marmite. Coffee jar. Sugar.
Strawberry jam. Mustard.
All written in my mother's hand.

My sister who learnt to write. Who wrote to me at college,
"My name is Katy. I am eleven. I like dogs and cats. You are my big
sister. When you come home you can talk to me."

PART THREE

They live in a bungalow. "No stairs to climb or fall down,
bungalows are best." My mother writes poems.
Bouncy happy poems about Hong Kong.
She remembers it all so well. When Grampa shot the cat
and Grandma's evening dress was silver grey,
and the nanny gave me eau de cologne. But that was Ceylon.

And my dad is her dad. I don't remember the day on the bay
when Pat swam out beyond the rock and they all called out.
Because I wasn't born yet. She gets confused.
"Have we had lunch? Is that the door bell?
And where's Katy?"

"She's with her carer, mum."
Their life is carers. One comes to get them up.
One comes to make their lunch. One comes to stay the night.
In case they wake. They can't be left.
"Is it Tuesday? Is it tea-time? Is that the door bell?
And where's Katy?"

Katy shuffles when she walks. She dribbles when she eats.
She smells of pee. She does jigsaws.
Thousand piece ones of sea and sky. This takes months.
She doesn't talk much except to say, "It hurts."
And, "Where's my mum?"

They cannot separate. Like Siamese twins
joined at the heart. One of them will die.

They're standing at the window. My mother and my sister.
My mother a bit bent now and peering hard.
She can't see too clearly,
and Katy, hanging on my mother's arm.
She's half a head smaller.
She sees me first. She calls out.
"Here she is. Here she is. Here's my big sister!"

THE GHOST IN CLAPHAM

My dad's been dead these thirty years but I saw him.
Outside a fruit and veg shop in Clapham.
I was by the crossing waiting for the lights to change
and he was there. On the other side, his back to me.
I knew it was him.
There was a cardigan he wore on Saturdays,
khaki, and faded
with leather patches on the sleeves.

The road was busy
and the cars and buses were streaming past.
I pressed the button again, hurry up, there's my dad!
My dead dad come back. I wasn't scared
but sort of impatient. I wanted to see
if it were really him. He looked so real.
The balding patch, the same square back.
The cardigan, the old man jeans.

Then I thought, oh come on, are you mad or what?
Why on earth would my dad come back as a ghost in Clapham?
Buying squashy plums opposite the underground?
He was a business man not a derelict.
He got his shirts made at Jermyn Street.
He bought cheese in Harrods.
He thought business class was slumming it.
He said, "Aim high and never accept second best."

And then I thought, this is a sign.
He died at sixty. Burned out by a stressful life
and a fast pace. This is a sign. Calm down. Enjoy
the Saturdays. Work is not everything. Remember
the good things like fresh apples and favourite cardigans.
I mustn't work so hard or I'll go nuts.
I must enjoy unexpected things like cheap fruit in Clapham.

And then I was sad,
and I felt the tears down my cheek. This was my dad.
Come back after thirty years. Isn't that what we all want
when someone dies? To see them once again?
Just to see them once?
To say, what did I want to say?
Dad. Dad. Why did you die? You never saw my life.
You never saw two of my sons. You missed my grown up life.

No, that wasn't it. Why should I scold him now?
The last thing he said to me was, "I've had enough."
Of pain and illness and the wait for death.
He didn't want to die. He didn't want to go.
He wanted to hang on until Christmas
and we would have the best one ever,
the one we would all remember because it was his last.

And all the presents we would have. And all our family
around the table, the way he wanted us to be.
And we would all go to midnight mass.
He died in September. On one of those early autumn days
when the sky was cobalt blue
and the leaves were tinged with gold.
And the last petals were falling off the climbing rose.
I took my baby son to the park.
We sat there and watched the clouds.

So, Dad, maybe it wasn't you.
When I crossed the road he had gone.
The man in the khaki cardigan.
But I like to think that you came back to make me stop.
And now, I never accept second best. I don't work too hard.
I have time for Saturdays, and clouds and squashy plums,
and ghosts
outside a fruit and veg shop in Clapham.

PRAYER TO IMPERFECTION

May I never be perfect.
Because I love mistakes and flaws in things.

Like the gumboots with a hole in.
Like the cake that went soggy in the middle.
Like the birthmark on the shoulder.
Like the three days it rained on your Devon home.

The gumboots with a hole in:
I only noticed they had a hole when I was half way
wading across the stream
and I would never have crossed that stream
unless I was wearing gumboots.

The cake that went soggy:
believe me it tasted better
with that uncooked cake, chocolate chip
and wooden spoon taste I hadn't tasted since I was eight.
I had forgotten it could taste so good.

The birthmark on the shoulder:
and how would I know you had a map of
France on your back until you took your shirt off?
And it didn't matter about the rain when we had
each other to explore.

Was it sorrow or was it joy?
We can talk right through the night.
Jam and bagels in the conservatory;
pink and red petunias and the spider's webs.
Does your loss feel as deep as mine?

May I never be perfect
because I love the jumps and turns.
The bust condom that was my youngest son.
The muddled up dates that were my middle one.
The what the hell I'm sure it's safe

that was my eldest one.
The relationship that ended and then I met a kinder man.
The party I didn't go to. The interview I missed.
The dress I ripped. The shoes that broke.
The luggage lost. The meal spoiled.
The exam I flunked. The ink ran out.
The hair cut horror. The bad smell date.
The clingy friend. The holiday flop.
My dad who died. The Downs Syndrome child.

May I never be perfect.
May I understand the wrinkles, the blots the rips.
My rocky landscape.
So unchartered. So unplanned.

WINTERWORLD

Streetsurfer down the frosty streets and you're cruising.
You have no plans. Sliding the cold sun in your hair,
you're unravelling the day
and knitting it into a bright jumper to keep you warm.

And the people you see on the street are a song in your head
with a beat like this, b'dum. B'dum. B'dum.
You breathe in their words icy like glass
and they melt and become a picture you're painting
of this day. Street surfer.

Dreamcatcher.
Tell me your dreams. Tell me your fantasies.
Touch each part of my everyday
and make me mind less that I live in it.
We need dreams.
Take your dreams and spread them out
to stain this grey and grainy place of bricks and streets
turning to brilliant opal shifting skies to walk through.
Streetsurfer. Dreamcatcher.

Earthshaker.
You're the bolt of lighting the corn flakes.
You're the blue cat on the doorstep.
You're the pair of socks that shouts, "Let's party!"
Light the fuse and stand back please
there's a crazy moment coming.
We're trying to sleep and you're still buzzing.
Cosmic bananas. Tantric Pyjamas.
Panoramas of dramaramas.
Set the alarm a rama rama rama,
and everything that begins with a 'W'.
Like wiped out and washed out and where's the day gone?
White frost patterns on the window in Winterworld.
Streetsurfer. Dreamcatcher. Earthshaker.

Heartbreaker.
You hurt people.
You spin so fast you don't see who you knock.
So busy taking it in. So busy with what you've made
you don't see what it cost.
It's wearing thin
and here comes the cold wind to freeze you
and the knock down people will turn away.
What did you eat today?
Can you remember what it feels like to eat good food?
Can you remember what it feels like
to wake up freshly slept?
Not as you usually are, wuzzy in your bed pit.
You're wearing thin. Skin on bone. Stretched paper
featherlight. And what's inside but mouthfuls of air?

Find a place. Another Winter. Of rotting leaves
and the smell of moss.
Even seeds are holding roots and you cannot remember
you need the earth as much as dreams.

Kneel now and push your fingers down
into the gritty soil as far as you can go.
Not so cold. Not so bleak as inside you.
Your darkness on the shortest day.
Feel inside you the small place you hide to stop hurting.
Long ago you locked away a tiny room
you need to open now and let the last big red sun stream in.
The sun that tells the seeds to wait and rest.

You need to wait and rest and feel yourself connect.
Streetsurfer. Dreamcather. Earthshaker.. Heart breaker.

We're all sleeping.
Waiting for the sun in Winterworld.

WEIRD WEATHER

Last April was so hot we swam in the river.
On the path was a puddle black with tadpoles.
Most were dead and smelled of rotting seaweed.
The others squirmed into the tyre tracks.

I wanted to walk to the river
and see anemones and wild garlic in the grass
not a puddle with black things.
Did they know that they were dying?

I dreamt that the ice age was coming.
Snow fields reached to the edge of the city.
An avalanche was predicted.
We panicked and ran from our houses.

My daughter was a fish girl
with pink gills like feathered seaweed.
I wrapped her in cellophane and put her in my pocket.
But I couldn't carry water in my pocket.

My son was four and was with his father.
The phones were down so I couldn't reach them.
I hoped his dad had wrapped him in an army blanket.
I hoped his dad had listened to the warnings.

I dreamt I saw my son in the street.
Standing still in the running people.
I was relieved because he was grown up.
He was wearing an army coat.

The young man wore a grey coat
but his face was cold with sadness.
He said, "Do they know they are dying?"
I woke up and I was crying.

MAY QUEEN

Her knicker lace was cow parsley.
Her blouse was the froth of the May tree.
Her skirt was patched with red campions and stitchwort
and she was dancing down the lanes.

Wild girl where are you now?
With your blue eyes and your careless laugh
and your apple blossom skin
and your pissy smell
and the mud splashed up your thighs
and your hair all anyhow.

You're in the deep woods stretched out
under the hazel and hornbeam.
The unfolding blanket of green
and the wet bed of bluebells.
The strange pale light over the bluebells.
And the song of a wren.
And the bluebells.

FOXY KNOXY

She didn't do it.
She was a late night party thing. Rummaging in dustbins
for sparkly bits of cloth.
Eating party leftovers. Half a sausage. A carrot stick.
Sticky chicken wings.

She wasn't dangerous. She was smoke and mirrors.
She put on a smile and showed her teeth.
Hitched up her skirt.
She wasn't dangerous but prowling.
She saw the mist before the dawn. She loved the mist.
She wasn't guilty. Only of being awake
when everyone else wasn't.
Why sleep when you can party?

Where's the party Foxy Knoxy?
And what are you doing at the bottom of my garden?
Hiding in the place where it all goes wild?
Do you love the dirty smell of compost?
Do you love the look of broken glass in the shed door?
The door you can't open because it's jammed shut.
Do you love the feel of squashy mud between your toes?

She saw her face in the broken window.
Red eyes. Sharp teeth. She was hungry and mad for it.
Another joint. Another blow and her mind spun.
She was howling.
A fox sounds like a baby tortured.

She did do it.
The back door was open and she crept in
up to the bedroom where the babies slept.
She did do it. The fox tore half the face off one.
The other, bit its arm to the bone.
Foxes bite the heads off chicken. Eat the breasts.
Scatter feathers in the coop.

She did do it.
Because she could. Blame the dope.
Blame the sex, or lack of it.
Blame the hate.

She did do it and she'll do it again.
Lock the back door. Shut the windows. Don't let her in.
She went down the garden behind the hedge.
And now we're scared.
Put down traps and poison meat. Reverse the hunting ban.
Someone's got a gun.
But she's still out there. You can kill a fox
but there'll always be another one.

OLD GREEN THINGS

Wednesdays are green. The sheen on a lilac leaf.
Those blousy flowers have dropped
and are scruffy seed heads.
But the leaf remains clean. Balanced one against the other
tangled in panicles of white hydrangeas.
Such smooth green hearts. Still romantic.

Sun through the nettles. Their leaves translucent, jagged.
A whole plot of nettles. Butterfly food.
Nettle beer. Nettle gruel.
This ragged vegetable crop. In March better than spinach.
The only vegetable you grow but the sun
doesn't bounce so gracefully off cabbage.

I am green. Ivy wrapped round a dead ash tree.
Slow forming, not seeking out sunlight but witnessing it.
My leaves dusty. Turning inwards I crawl up the wall
and inside to mangle bright things, like geraniums
and block the windows.

A green stain on a bath tub.
Years and years and years and years of water dripping
the trace element of copper.
Green pipes corroded and the wet
mess soaked up by a shaggy bathmat.

I am sly. Insidious.
Old green thing.

A lilac tree when the bloom has gone.
An ivy plant creeping round the mossy pots.
A tired nettle bouncing off the sun.

ELDERFLOWERS

Elderflowers are creamy white.
Tiny flowers. Exquisite embroidery on
a fine corsage of a wedding dress slipped on in midsummer.
Where are the bridesmaids?
Where is the groom?

She put on her creamy dress
and looked at the clock, nearly noon.
Her mother was out, exams were over,
no school. Just this empty shell of summer.
Next year uni. Then what? Another blank. She was bored.
Up the road was a farm.
Fat guy. Fat wife. Smelled of cheese.
A skinny son with acne.
He looked through the hedge when she lay in the sun.
She knew that. Sometimes she took off her top.
Her mother said, "Anne, please cover up."
What did she know?
Hadn't had a man since Dad left.

She was bored.
Why did they live out here in a shabby old cottage
where nothing worked? Why not a town?
At least there would be stuff going on.
But not Newton Abbot. She'd rather be dead.
Her mum was at Asda, "Anne, could you wash the floor?"
For fuck's sake. You could wash that
floor a hundred times and it wouldn't look clean.
Why was everything broken? The hot tap, and the cupboard
door was falling off.

Twenty past twelve. He said, "I'll be there at one."
She brushed her hair. It was brown and shone.
She had hazel eyes and her skin was gold
except the white bits where her pants were.

She put on lipstick. Too red. Too tarty.
She wiped it off. A red smear along the back of her hand.
She looked at the clock. Twenty to one.

Elderflowers smell sweet
like marshmallows or candy floss
but more lingering, more pungent,
not like honeysuckle, not so strong
or roses, doesn't last so long.
Smells like spunk.

She smelled the rose by the front door.
Prince Camille de Rohan. Grand name!
"All the roses have names," said her mum.
This one was maroon, almost purple,
crumpled and curled. Bunched up petals and plump.
She wanted to smell like that.
Grown up.

She walked, trying to look nonchalant.
She liked that word. Nonchalant.
Down the road to the lane.
Nobody saw. Not the farmer's wife. Thank God.
And the son was at school. Lee? Who cares?
The hedges were high. On the banks were foxgloves,
naval worts. Pointy things.
When you live in the country you know the names.
Yes, it was pretty.
And elderflowers in the hedge. They smelled like wine.
She began to run.

Elderflowers are soft like expensive lace on an underslip.
Soadsuds in a bubble bath in a posh hotel.
Pillow lace. Muslin curtains
with a faint pattern stitched in.
And clouds. When she was young she used to lie on the grass
and pretend to touch the clouds. And blow them away.
Puff. Puff. Blow the clouds away. Puff.

She was running down the lane. Down a green tunnel.
Just skimming nettles, avens, dog mercury.
Wished she hadn't worn sandals.
It was cooler in here.
Like a watershoot she used to love in the pool.
And there were elderflowers
along the hedge arching over her.
Elderflowers above her head.
The lane was muddy. Today it wasn't.
Her feet crunched. Ferns. Ivy. Brambles. Scratchy.
People didn't come down here. Too overgrown.
Didn't come down here. Didn't go anywhere.

Elderflowers make good pancakes.
Mixed in with yellow batter. Cooked in butter.
Served with cream. Cream and lemon. Cream and sugar.
Bad food. Naughty food.
Elderflower fizz.
Fermenting in the cupboard until the winter.
Open the bottle. Smell the summer.
Drink. Drink. Drink. Drink.
It makes you giddy and giggly and hot.

She stopped. The lane opened into a field.
A small field not much used.
Buttercups and feathery grass
down the track to the boathouse by the lake.
No boats. No canoes.
But boxes of flowerpots and a rusty lawnmover.
He came here to be quiet, he said.
He came here to think, he said.

She stopped and caught her breath
and tried to look nonchalant.
Hard, with her hair messed up and her face all hot.
Why did she run?
In the village the clock struck one.

She brushed her fingers through her hair.
There were elderflower petals in her hair.
Was he there?
And pushed the door.

The smell of hot wood and creosote.
A startled spider ran down a web.
A flimsy funnel on the window pane.
He said, "So, you've come again."
His eyes were hazel just like hers.
There was silver grey in his hair.
He was married and forty one. An architect once.
Wasn't working now. Got depressed.
She undressed.

Elderflowers along the hedge.
A man's hand on a woman's breast.
A man's body blurring hers.
A crumpled dress on a dirty floor.
The creaking floor of an old shed.
And the lingering smell of elderflowers.

DAISIES

Daisies on a lawn. White petals edged with pink.
Bright in the sun. Buttercups and dandelions in the field.
And daisies. Tough stalks and a ring of leaves.
On the lawn under the apple tree.

Teenage girls doing back flips.
Bright eyes and messed up hair. Bikini tops and tiny shorts.
Puppy limbs and pink skin. Then flopped
in the shade under apple blossom.
Making jewellery. A bracelet. A necklace.
A four foot long fragile daisy string.

Who made the first daisy chain?
A mother and a stone age child?
They had no time with the scrape of flint on pig skin.
Or in the woods finding haws.
Foot prints in the mud.
Daisies are not forest flowers

Daisies grow in farmer's fields.
Mown by sheep and cut with blades.
Two farmer's daughters. Not yet wed.
Stopped making cheese and bashing dough.
Flopped on the grass under the apples trees.
Picked a daisy. Split the stalk. Threaded it through.
Then another. A whispered secret.
Too soon shrivelled. Too soon spoiled.

JUNE DAY

10am.
Take off your coat.
You don't need it today.
The sun is out and the heat is up.
Let's leave behind the queue to Tescos
and the tail back to Bude, and walk along the ditch
on the track where the sheep walk
now newly nude and skittish in their summer skin,
to the hay store where you say a barn owl's nesting.

The village is a sleepy string along the ridge
but we are far below with the meadow sweet
and the elderflowers and the flash of dragon flies.
Far below the petrol lawnmowers and the whiff of barbeques.
Lamb kebabs and onion rings.

The ruined barn, where the light shines through the rafters.
An old beam's fallen in.
We push along a fence of nettles.
Don't get stung.

There's no owls but swallows skim
chattering to their young.
There's no hay but dust and nettles
and rotting wood.

Someone will buy this place. Do it up in glass and steel.
Sheer off the greeny coat. But not now.
Keep it like this.
These massive stones and dust and nettles

2pm.
Take off your shirt.
You don't need it today.
Let's flop on your lawn and count the clouds.
There aren't any. Not even cirrus. Not a wisp
just the contrails of a plane coming back to Heathrow.
Your lawn is not a lawn it's a biomass of plantains
and daises and buttercups.
The vegetables patch has long gone
to brambles and honeysuckle.
It's only a garden because you say so.
Too hot for lunch. Just a cheese sandwich and an apple.
Chuck the core into the hedge.
There's a tractor in the lane.
The plane has gone.

8pm.
Take off your pants.
You don't need them today.
Because we are in the secret pond behind the apple tree.
It's an old bath on bricks.
Filled with a hosepipe and warmed by a fire underneath.
You and me, pink as shorn sheep in a sheep wash.
It's not erotic. It's animal. Get hot. Lie in Water.
Feel my skin crinkle. Listen to the fire pop.
No, it's not animal. It's vegetable.
The water bubbles. We are soup.
Sweet potatoes in this murky brew
falling apart and becoming thick.
Did you say something? No.
Look, there's the first star. And another.
Altair. Deneb. Vega.

A WET SUMMER

The road's a river past your door.
The garden's turned to mush.
The snails leave trails in the conservatory
and I have just squeezed one pint of water from my sock.

I thought it was the morning but it's tea time.
There has been no sun for three days now.
The light is green like underwater.
The hills and fields are lost in wet.

Let's do nothing but drink sauvignon blanc
and chuck damp logs on the smoking fire,
or not get up but stay in bed, compare our toes,
fingernails, noses. This isn't a holiday.

This is the summer washing down the drainpipe.
What's that weird yellow thing? It's the sun.
No, it's not. It just got blotted by the next grey cloud
dumping hailstones on the thatch.

And now the afternoon drips to night.
Oh, we're having sex again.
It's so dark I can't see the furniture or your face
but I can feel you. I can feel you.
Did I think I could escape from myself?
Inside me is an ocean, indigo and deep,
unexplored, forgotten, still.

There is no hope for us when
we have experienced everything
that can go wrong in relationships;
divorce, betrayal, disappointment, death.
I have strange dreams.
My past lovers all line up and laugh at me.
Your dead wife stands naked on the grass
in the moonlight. I can't hear what she's saying.
I think it is, 'Don't go there.'

But I remember sun. Running in the sun,
along a hot, white sand beach
straight into the water. Straight into the waves.
Did you ever swim right out
beyond the waves, beyond the stack?
Then turn round and look back at
the people like spots of colour on the strand.
And as you basked in a curve of warmth
feel underneath you the heavy weight
of cold dark water. Indigo and deep.
Unexplored. Forgotten. Still.

BATS

The migraine has lodged behind one eye
and in the other the vision's fractured with the light.
I'm lying on your bed waiting for sleep or relief.
Sounds are louder, more extreme.
My breathing. The squeak of the springs.
You outside with the petrol strimmer.

The phone rings. It's your friend.
She's got bed bugs because you gave her
a cupboard infested with the things.

The strimmer screams
and eighteen years of neglect
is starting to be a vegetable patch.
I try to think of something peaceful,
like cabbages and carrots,
in weedless well hoed lines.
There's an ash tree in the middle.
That will have to go. Where's the chainsaw?

The phone rings. No. No. No.
They are not bed bugs! They are bat bugs!
Because the cupboard was in your barn where the bats are.
She's sent you pictures in an e-mail,
she found it on the internet,
and her whole house is crawling.

The strimmer whines. The phone rings.
Now her mattress is on the street, and the cupboard,
and where are they all going to sleep?
Her landlady is sobbing, and so is she,
it's going to cost hundreds to sort it out
and who will pay? You will.
You must ring the council, and her landlady and Rentokill.

I put a pillow on my head.
I want a real crisis. Your sister's got cancer.
Your wife died eighteen years ago.
Next week you have a blood test.
My mother's got Alzheimer's.

I make it downstairs
and flop in a garden chair.
You are dirty and raddled
but sort of pleased. With nettles in your hair.
The plot's been flattened.

We sit and watch the evening come
and bats darting through the trees.
Bats. Pipistrelles. Expert divers and swoopers.
High pitched squealers. Scratchy claws.
Ugly faces, pointy teeth and floppy wings.
Little things.

SUMMER'S OVER

Summer's over and the gales blow in from the west.
Bend the hollyhocks and chuck plums on the lawn.
Apples are falling but not sweet enough to eat
their white taste makes my eyes water.

I have woken up to a fresh wind and a bright sky
and the clouds being punched
and a day when I am holding my breath
waiting for more bad news.
But the storm has passed and there is only debris.
Twigs. Leaves. A dustbin lid. A skid mark on a road.
A shoe in a ditch.

The last flowers on the climbing rose are brown.
My mother's hands with skin like tea stained silk
She folds up newspapers in boxes.
Memories are being stored.

CHRISTMAS SPIRIT

I don't like the run up to Christmas.
All that brash tangle of tinsel and baubles.
The supermarket scrum and the noise.
Jing a ling ling the sleigh bells ring
don't they know it's Christmas time?

I remember it quieter.
A smell of greenery in the living room.
Wrapping up presents in front of a fire;
the hiss of gas and the crackle of paper.
A child's eyes when they saw the lit up tree.

What is the Christmas spirit? I think I felt it
up on Troopers Hill after the snow fall.
And Oh, I know, I know, I know
that a city in the snow is a snarled mess
of tired drivers and slipping pedestrians,
but it didn't look like that.

The snow was still fresh
in the hollows of the old mine works.
And below us every roof was white.
Every office window shone.
Every council house garden an untouched space.
All around us the kids sped down
impossible slopes on bits of plastic.
Everybody was laughing.
And we were laughing. Trying to work out
what were those shining distant hills.
The Quantocks? Exmoor?
Did it matter? They were thick with snow

and radiant. Almost blue.
Shining distant hills.

ACKNOWLEDGEMENTS

Set No Limits and *What's the Story Morning Bollocks* were featured in the film *Bristol Poetry Whores on Tour*. with Julian Ramsey-Wade and Ethos Sphere. Directed by David Greenhalgh for H.T.V 1997

Let Me Be was published in *Oral: Poems, songs, lyrics and the like*. Sceptre 1999

This Poem was published in *Velocity*. Apples and Snakes. Black Spring Press 2003

Wasting Time, The Seventies Were Crap, Shopping and *You Are The One for Me* were part of *Three Night Stand* with David Johnson and Peter Hunter 2004

Liar was adapted into a short film by China Moo Young. 2005. Screened at film festivals including Cannes, Raindance, San Francisco and Hamburg. New Producers Alliance Best Shorts Finalist and Runner up Winner 2006. Distributed by Future Shorts.

I Want To Be A Bitch, The Quiet Life, Cemetery Road, Half Life and *My Life as a Porn Movie* were written for the *Temptation* tour. Apples and Snakes 2005

I was Born in a Strange Country, Family Prayers, My Mother and My Sister, The Ghost in Clapham and *Prayer to Imperfection* were part of *Flash* with Sarah-Jane Arbury, Anna Freeman and Glen Carmichael. 2010-11

Take Me To The City was one of the poems chosen for adaptation in the *Liberated Words Poetry Film Festival* 2012. The selected films were made by Jon Conway of Imprint and Helen Dewberry.